"Unto You and Your Children"

"Unto You and Your Children"

The Promises of the Covenant

A Primer

Larry E. Ball, M.Div.

VICTORIOUS HOPE
PUBLISHING

Fountain Inn, South Carolina 29644

"Proclaiming the kingdom of God and teaching those things which concern
the Lord Jesus Christ, with all confidence."
(Acts 28:31)

Unto You and Your Children: The Promises of the Covenant
by Larry E. Ball
Copyright © 2016 by Larry E. Ball

Unless otherwise noted, Scripture references are taken from the New American Standard Bible, (c) 1960, 1962, 1963, 1968, 1971, 1972, 1973, 1975, 1977 by The Lockman Foundation. Used by permission.

Published by Victorious Hope Publishing
P.O. Box 1874
Fountain Inn, South Carolina 29644

Website: www.VictoriousHope.com

Printed in the United States of America

ISBN: 978-0-9826206-9-4

VICTORIOUS HOPE PUBLISHING is committed to producing Christian educational materials for promoting the whole Bible for the whole of life. We are conservative, evangelical, and Reformed and are committed to the doctrinal formulation found in the Westminster Standards.

Dedication

This book is dedicated to my dear wife
Brenda
who is indeed a faithful covenant mother

TABLE OF CONTENTS

INTRODUCTION

This is a book about the place of children in the church. How should we view our children as they are being raised in the church? Should we call them Christians or not? Are they unbelievers until they make a profession of faith? Should we baptize them as infants or wait until they publicly profess their own faith? I will attempt to answer these and many other related questions in this book.

It is sad that so many children grow up in the church and then leave the church as they grow into adulthood. From statistics I have read the modern church has a problem retaining her children. It seems that as soon as some young people learn to drive a car or go off to college, they leave the church. In addition, it is important to understand that when we lose our children we ultimately lose our grandchildren too. It is like a domino effect. It is heart-breaking.

Many Christian parents live in constant fear that their children will leave the faith. However, it does not need to be this way. I know many Christian families who see their children grow up and become an integral part of the church. There is a reason for this. They are doing something right. I believe there is hope, and I believe that much of what I say in this book can mitigate this distressing loss of the children of the church. I believe that the normal expectation of parents should be to see their children continue in the faith as adults and even watch them flourish as they follow Christ. Ultimately, the impact of losing our children also affects our nation. As families become de-Christianized, our nation loses one of its most valuable resources.

Regarding salvation, modern Christians tend to think in terms of personal relationships only. However, the Bible clearly teaches that God's blessings and curses are also corporate, and even as important, they are also generational. Family and societal *world-views* (from the German term "Weltanschauung") and their resulting lifestyles are transferred from one generation to another; and often if there is no restraining grace on God's part, each generation becomes worse. Sin only begets more sin. Children may suffer for the sins of their fathers up to three and four generations (great-great-grandchildren). The stranglehold or iron grip of sin in the family and in society is very difficult to break from generation to generation.

Nevertheless, the good news (the gospel) is that it can be broken. God can intervene with his grace and change everything, not just for individuals but for families and nations. The Bible teaches that God does bless the children of godly parents up to a thousand generations (the word *thousand* is a metaphor for the word *multitude*). The first commandment says that God visits the "iniquity of the fathers on the children, on the third and fourth generations of those who hate Me, but showing lovingkindness to thousands [of generations], to those who love Me and keep My commandments" (Ex. 20:5–6).[1]

I once was asked by a visitor to my church (where I was the pastor for thirty-one years) what our church had to offer him and his family, especially his children. I told him that we did not offer a youth minister, a gymnasium, or other typical ministries that exist in many evangelical churches, but I did tell him that there was one thing we could offer him. I told him that if he became an integral part of our church then he would not lose his children to the world as they grew into adulthood. Of course, I could not promise a one-hundred percent success rate, but I could testify that nearly all of our children grew into mature Christians as adults. A child leaving the faith as an adult was the exception to the rule. We were doing something right. In essence, as you will see in this book, I believe

---

[1] All Scripture texts will be from the New American Standard Bible (NASB).

that one of the main reasons we were retaining our children was our view of the covenant.

I believe that critical to answering numerous questions about the place of children in the church, there is first a need to understand the concept of a covenant. The word covenant pervades the entire Bible. It is used in the Scriptures over three hundred times. Jesus describes his relationship to the New Testament church using the concept of a covenant. For example, when he instituted the Lord's Supper he referred to the covenant. "And in the same way He *took* the cup after they had eaten, saying, 'This cup which is poured out for you is the new covenant in My blood'" (Luke 22:20). Jesus assumed that his disciples understood the meaning of the word covenant. We need such knowledge too. The church is in a covenant relationship with God.

In days when the church seems to be downplaying denominational differences, it may seem unnecessary that I would write a book on an issue that has divided the church for centuries. Doctrinal differences between various denominations only divide, and some people would say that it might be well if we just avoid that which divides. Certainly, every Christian should pursue unity as much as possible. For many of you, the best way to keep peace in the family is to hide this book when particular relatives come to visit.

Yet, every Christian must come to some conclusion on such issues as infant baptism (which I prefer to call covenant baptism). If you have children, either you have had your children baptized or you have not. Your action reveals your doctrinal views or at least your willingness to be in subjection to a spouse who holds to these beliefs. The intent of this book is not to further divide the church but rather to demonstrate the importance of understanding the covenant. It is important to capture the meaning of covenant baptism and its impact on how we raise our children. I don't see the church erasing this controversy from its existence anytime soon.

Church leaders will always have strong convictions and will lead their flock in the direction of their personal views. This is true of me too.

Even though there have been many other books written on this subject, what was readable years ago may not be so readable today. Though the arguments do not vary much over time, the mindset of the Christian does. My attempt in this book is to address the old arguments in new ways that the modern Christian can understand. Some of the older books are just too complicated for most Christians. They also assume that the reader understands some basic principles about the nature of conversion which may not always be true. My niche in the world of writing is making complicated ideas simple. I like to go back and start from original assumptions in order to properly develop a subject. I have an urge to go back to the beginning and start with definitions. Maybe I get this compulsion from having studied mathematics in college. I believe I can reduce the complexities of the scholar (oftentimes found in long and laborious books) to the level of the man in the pew.

This is why this book and my previous book[2] are called primers. A primer is an introduction to a topic. It tries to present something difficult in a plain and simple way so the reader might understand complicated ideas. A primer is usually a short book, and this will be a short book. I don't consider myself a scholar. I have to study long and hard to discern what more gifted men are saying, but usually after a certain amount of time, I finally understand. As I learn what others are teaching and then filter it through my own simple mind, God has given me a passion to take it to the man in the pew in ways he can understand. Most people don't read lengthy books anymore. In this short book I want to capture the minds of busy people for just a few hours.

---

[2] *Blessed Is He Who Reads: A Primer on the Book of Revelation* (2d. ed.: Fountain Inn, S.C.: Victorious Hope, 2015).

I have dealt with a number of people who were raised in the Presbyterian Church where covenant baptism was practiced, but they never really understood what they were doing. Among some parents there was always a bit of doubt in their minds as to why the sacrament was being administered to their children. In addition, I have dealt with those who were raised in other denominations and then thrust by marriage into churches that baptize babies. They were raised to believe in "believer's baptism," and then when their own children came along, their spouses expected them to support the practice of their new church. It was very difficult for them to have their children baptized when they had been raised to think negatively of it.

If you came from a non-covenant background, having your children baptized may test your willingness to be in subjection to the views of a spouse who believes in covenant baptism. It is also difficult when Grandpa and Grandma, who maybe were also confused about covenant baptism, come to the special baptismal service for their newly-born grandchildren.

Other men with views similar to mine have not tended to be active in defending our views. We have not given our people a good defense (or even a good offense) in handling opposing views. Members of our churches are often left perplexed. As Gary North has said for years, "You can't fight something with nothing." Covenant baptism in many denominations has become a tradition without a theological understanding of why the church believes in it and practices it. The practice is misunderstood and badly abused in some circles. This may be one reason why the pews are so empty in many Presbyterian churches. This book seeks to correct those deficiencies. It seeks to demonstrate the biblical basis for what we do. Hopefully it will give meaning and joy to those who participate in the sacrament of covenant baptism.

Understanding both the place of children in the church and the importance of covenant baptism is a little like climbing a mountain.

Before you can enjoy the view from the top of the mountain, you must first climb up the difficult pathways and push your way through the brush below. Before I became convinced of the legitimacy of covenant baptism, I first had to wrestle with other doctrines in the Bible. It's the other doctrinal beliefs we derive from the Bible that are sometimes most important in understanding covenant baptism.

John Crawford makes this clear in the title of his book — *Baptism Is Not enough: How Understanding God's Covenant Explains Everything.*[3] I do believe that simply quoting certain Scriptures establishes a solid argument for covenant baptism, but that position will become clearer as we understand these other doctrinal issues first. The issue before us is greater than just the baptism of infants. Covenant baptism is only one part of a particular approach to the Scriptures. This approach is often embodied in what is called Covenant Theology. As you will see, it is connected with other biblical doctrines about the very nature of God and also how God saves Christians.

Before we look at the covenant and how it affects the raising of children in the church, we need to get some other things right first. It may surprise you that about half of this book is not about the covenant. I deal with a number of other issues first. As I mentioned in the previous paragraph, this is because understanding the covenant is dependent upon a clear understanding of other doctrines. Only as you understand the basics of the gospel and how God converts his people, can you begin to see how the covenant works in the lives of your children.

In Chapter 1 of this book I will revisit the meaning of the gospel. This is of primary importance. I'm not sure everyone is on the same page when we talk about the gospel. I will define some important

---

[3] John Crawford, *Baptism Is Not Enough: How Understanding God's Covenant Explains Everything* (Powder Springs, Geo.: American Vision, 2013).

terms in Chapter 2 that I will be using in subsequent chapters. We will analyze the meaning of such terms as regeneration and conversion. I am afraid that even though we all may be reading in the same language, we still may be using different definitions for some of these biblical terms. I will give a short testimony to my own conversion in Chapter 3, as well as deal with various experiences of conversion described in the Bible. I struggled a great deal over understanding my own conversion, and I believe that many others will resonate with my experience.

Understanding these first three chapters will be very important to understanding the nature of a covenant and how it affects our families. Chapters 4 and 5 will be devoted to the concept of a covenant itself with a rationale for covenant baptism. Then finally, we will consider some practical issues on how to raise our children in light of their covenant relationship with God (Chapter 6).

As I previously mentioned, this is a short book. It is an introduction to the topic of how the covenant affects our children, and I hope it will stimulate the reader to pursue the topic in more depth. May God use this book to help those who struggle with this important issue.

Larry E. Ball
Kingsport, Tennessee
January 2016

1
WHAT IS THE GOSPEL?

Before we consider the place of children in the church and the nature of covenant baptism, I think first it is important that we revisit the meaning of the gospel. Being part of the covenant does not negate believing in the gospel. We have to get this right. In days of so much confusion, even in evangelical churches, I am convinced that Christians need to understand exactly what the gospel is. This will impact how we deal with our children.

The greatest benefit of the Protestant Reformation of the sixteenth century was that the gospel was rediscovered. As a result of the corruption of the Roman Catholic Church over a period of hundreds of years, the gospel had in essence been lost. The Protestant Reformation was a major event in the history of the Christian Church.

We live in another day where there is a great amount of confusion in regard to the definition of the gospel. The previous confusion in the Roman Catholic Church resulted from a strong centralized church. Ironically, today this confusion results from a great multiplicity of churches, each seeking to define the gospel in their own way. In a sense we have gone from one pope to thousands of popes. The definition of the gospel has become so confused that, in my opinion, few people actually understand what it is. Read carefully. In an age where we hear so much about the gospel, I am convinced that few people really know what it is. From knowing people in various theological camps including liberalism, fundamentalism, evangelicalism, Pentecostalism, and others, I am afraid the gospel has been lost again. I believe another Reformation is needed in the twenty-first century.

My attempt here in this chapter will be to define the gospel. I believe it is one of the greatest needs of the church today. As I mentioned in the Introduction, we expect covenant children to believe the gospel. The covenant does not deny the call to believe the gospel. Without a biblical understanding of the gospel, what do we have to offer to our children or to a dying world? How do we know that we really have been saved by the gospel, if we are not clear as to what it is? When we offer a false gospel (with good intentions) to the world, we only do great harm and further alienate those who hear it. Understanding the gospel is an important preliminary to understanding the broader issue of the covenant and our children.

What the Gospel Is Not

In order to clarify what the gospel is, I first will deal with what the gospel is not. I believe that by uncovering the errors of modern day false gospels, I can better explain what the gospel actually is. Often, we can better understand truth, by first looking at error. The light shines brighter against the background of darkness. I will list several popular gospels that are prominent misconceptions of the biblical gospel.

Misconception #1

The gospel is not believing that the events surrounding Christ have historical significance or that they did actually happen. The facts of history do support that there really was a Jesus who lived two thousand years ago. Many in other religions will admit to the historicity of many biblical accounts and even have a zealous interest in these events. Yet, having an interest, or even having made a trip to the "Holy Land," does not in any way make you a Christian or a child of God. Believing that Jesus did actually live and that the Bible is a true account of his life is not the gospel.

Misconception #2

The gospel is not that God loves the whole world and there are many ways to God. This gospel, popular in liberal circles, teaches that Jesus just happens to be the best way to God. They teach that there are many ways to God including Buddhism, Hinduism, Islam, Judaism, and Christianity. This definition is often heard from the mouths of modern politicians living in a pluralistic society, such as candidates for high offices. Their "civil religion" prayer meetings generally include a variety of religious leaders in order not to offend any particular religion.

As long as the name "God" is reverenced, then it is believed that such people must be included among those who are defined as the children of God. This is American Civil Religion, and not Christianity. It is certainly not the gospel. Jesus clearly said in John 14:6, "I am the way, and the truth, and the life; no one comes to the Father but through me." Christianity is by its very nature exclusive. Those outside of Christ are not children of God.

Misconception #3

The gospel is not that God is love and if you try to live the best you can, hopefully God will let you into heaven. The Bible says in Isaiah 64:6, "For all of us have become like one who is unclean. And all our righteous deeds are like a filthy garment..." Paul says in Romans 3:10, "There is none righteous, not even one; there is none who understands, there is none who seeks for God..." The Book of Galatians makes it clear that "as many as are of the works of the Law are under a curse..." (Galatians 3:10). Good works cannot make one ready to meet God and be accepted into heaven. God is holy. God only accepts perfection, and no man has lived a perfect life, except Jesus Christ. Apart from the gospel, one sin, one miscue, one omission of duty, disqualifies every man from being accepted as a child of God.

Misconception #4

The gospel is not that I am a child of God because I am a member of a Church. Church membership never made anyone a child of God. Please don't misunderstand me here. Church membership is important. The writers of the Westminster Confession of Faith in the seventeenth century said, "there is ordinarily no salvation outside of the visible church."[4] Those who are children of God are faithful members of a visible church (one with a name, and people in it with elders, deacons, sacraments, etc.), but church membership in itself does not make you a child of God. There are many church members sitting in the pews of churches today who have no idea what the gospel is.

Misconception #5

The gospel is not the feeling that I feel like I am saved. To say, "I'm sure I am saved," is not the gospel. Feelings are important in understanding the gospel, but just because a man may have assurance that he is saved, does not mean that he is saved or understands the gospel. The assurance of salvation and knowing the gospel, are two different things. Many people with assurance of salvation are indeed Christians; however, on the other hand, there

---

[4] *Westminster Confession of Faith*, The Publications Committee of the Presbyterian Church of Scotland (1976 Edition), Chapter XXV, Section II.

are many who do not doubt their salvation who have false assurance. They do not understand the gospel. They identify good feelings or some unfounded assurance with the gospel itself. This is not the gospel.

Paul encouraged the Corinthians in 2 Corinthians 13:5, to "Test yourselves to see if you are in the faith; examine yourselves! Or do you not recognize this about yourselves, that Jesus Christ is in you – unless indeed you fail the test." In other words, many people feel saved, or believe they are children of God, and yet do not know what the gospel is. I may feel healthy, but I may be dying of cancer. Feelings are not the final test of whether one believes the gospel. Likewise, there are many people who constantly doubt their own salvation who understand and believe the gospel. This is sad too, but it is true.

Misconception #6

The gospel is not that I know that I am a child of God because God has answered my prayers. God does answer the prayers of his children, but this in itself is no guarantee that you know what the gospel is. God, because He is good, has been good to many people who are not even Christians. As a matter of fact, those who are not the children of God oftentimes find life generally much better than those who are the children of God. "Life is good" may be their motto, but this in no way indicates that they know God. The Psalmist found this a great dilemma when he asked why the righteous suffer and the wicked prosper (Psalm 73). An easy life and outward, physical blessings are not final, conclusive evidence that you are a child of God or that you believe the gospel.

Misconception #7

The gospel is not that I have done great things for God. A man can preach from the pulpit, be an elder in the Church, even perform miracles in the name of Christ, and still not be a child of God. Jesus said in Matthew 7:22–23, "Many will say to Me on that day, 'Lord, Lord, did we not prophesy in Your name, and in Your name cast out demons, and in Your name perform many miracles?' And then I will declare to them, I never knew you, 'DEPART FROM ME, YOU WHO PRACTICE LAWLESSNESS.'"

Misconception #8

The gospel is not walking an aisle in a revival meeting or a church service. Just because you responded to a preacher's call to come to the front of the Church, or came to the altar, does not mean you either understand or believe in the gospel. Many preachers have a psychological quota they feel they must meet in order to consider themselves successful. Many people have been manipulated into responding to an altar call who do not understand or believe the gospel. Now, you may have walked the aisle and may indeed be a Christian. I am just saying that walking the aisle in a revival meeting does not mean you understand the gospel.

Misconception #9

The gospel is neither having decided for Jesus nor having invited Jesus into your heart. Neither of these acts on the part of man indicates that you understand or know the gospel. You may have done this and you may be a Christian. However, there are thousands of people who have decided for Jesus or invited Jesus into their heart, but do not either understand or believe the gospel.

Nowhere in the Bible is the gospel ever described as deciding for Jesus or inviting Jesus into your heart. The text in Revelation 3:20 where Jesus stands at the door and knocks is written to the Christians in the church at Laodicea and not to those outside of the church.

Misconception #10

The gospel is not a matter of simply being baptized. As we shall see, baptism is very important in identifying with Christ, but baptism without understanding the gospel will not give you the forgiveness of sins.

Preliminary Conclusion

None of these acts or beliefs, although some are part and parcel with believing the gospel, is the gospel. None of them give final evidence that you either understand or believe the gospel. That is why I said previously that I believe the gospel has been lost today. We have many modern false substitutes in the modern age.

What the Gospel Is

First Premise

What then is the gospel? Let me describe the gospel to you. First, to understand the gospel, you must believe that you are in a hole so deep, that there is nothing you can do to pull yourself out. There is nothing you can do to save yourself. As one of my former seminary professors once said, your analysis of your condition is similar to that of being at the bottom of a pit a hundred miles deep with walls covered with slippery oil. There is no ladder or rope, and there is no one within a thousand miles to hear your cry. The hole is full of poisonous snakes. You are there because of sin. You have broken God's law; you have failed to measure up to his standards, and he is angry with you. You are hopeless, and you are in an impossible situation. Ephesians 2:1–3 describes our situation before we become Christians, "And you were dead in your trespasses and sins, in which you formerly walked according to the course of this world, according to the prince of the power of the air, of the spirit that is now working in the sons of disobedience. Among them we too all formerly lived in the lusts of our flesh, indulging the desires of the flesh and of the mind, and were by nature children of wrath, even as the rest." We were dead men under the power of sin, not sick men who can in some sense help ourselves. Without the hope of the gospel we are dead men. Dead men are hopeless men. They have no ability to give themselves life, or to repair their dead bodies.

Second Premise

Secondly, to understand the gospel, we must understand that we are not able to decide for Jesus. As I heard one man say it once, it is not even a question of whether we decided for Jesus, but rather a question of whether Jesus decided for us. The evidence that Jesus has decided for us is that we have been born again. As sinners without God, we need to be born again. Jesus said in John 3:7–9, "Do not be amazed that I said to you, 'You must be born again.' The wind blows where it wishes and you hear the sound of it, but do not know where it comes from and where it is going; so is everyone who is born of the Spirit. Nicodemus answered and said to Him, 'How can these things be?'" John also tells us in John 1:12–13, "But as many as received Him, to them He gave the right to become the children of God, even those who believe in His name, who were born not of blood, nor of the will of the flesh, nor of the will of man, but of God."

The Critical Point

My friend, the point is this, that you cannot understand or believe the gospel until there has been removed from you every possibility of your contributing, adding, or complementing in any way the work of Christ as he saves his people. To believe the gospel you must first be driven a hundred miles into a deep dark hole. You have sinned against God, broken his law, and his wrath abides on you. You have no ability to save yourself; you have no ability to bring yourself out of that deep hole. You are in a hopeless situation. If you do not see this, it is my opinion (and I believe also the opinion of great men like Calvin, Luther, and Spurgeon) that you do not know what the gospel is.

At this point you may ask, "What can I do?" The answer is, you can do nothing! The biblical question is, "What must I do?" (Acts 2:37). This is the way a man must ask the question. The word "can" assumes that you have the ability to do something. The word "must" assumes that you have no ability, but that you do have responsibility. You are indeed responsible to believe the gospel. Believing the gospel is evidence that God has changed your heart.

Flee to Christ

The answer to the question as to the nature of the gospel, is that in recognizing your terrible condition, you must flee to Christ and plead for His mercy. You must trust that he is able to deliver you out of your present condition. You must hope in his power, his promises, and his work on the cross to forgive you of your sins. You must believe that he can pull you out of your present condition, and set you on a new pathway of serving and loving Him. Only he can do this by his power. You have nothing to add to his power. You are not his co-pilot. Your trust is not in yourself, or in how much faith you have, but in his power to save you. Only he can clean up your nasty heart. Only he can plead your case before the Heavenly Father. Only Christ by his death on the cross can forgive you of your sins. Believing in Christ is not the work of your own free-will, but evidence that God has changed your heart and given you the desire to flee to Christ. Much of the confusion that you may have at this point hopefully will be cleared up in the next chapter as I deal with the issue of conversion.

Justified by Faith

Only Christ can save us and make us children of God. We have no ability to do so ourselves. All we can do is cry out for His mercy, asking for grace to trust in his power and promises. As we flee to Christ, hoping, trusting, and committing ourselves to him alone who has the ability to save us, then we are justified by that faith. We are declared righteous on the basis of his life and work on the cross. Romans 5:1 tells us, "Therefore having been justified by faith, we have peace with God through our Lord Jesus Christ…" Like Abraham of old, we are reckoned as being righteous because we believe and trust in the promises of God (Romans 4:3). We need perfection to be accepted into Heaven. None of us have it. We must be justified or declared right with God. Justification is a legal declaration of God whereby he declares those who put their faith in him to be righteous (perfect). We are *legally* sinless even though we are still *actually* sinful. Justification is therefore a gracious act of God toward sinners, and can only be received by faith alone.

The righteousness of Christ, which is perfect, is charged to our account, even though we did not earn it or deserve it. It is ours by grace, and it makes us acceptable (justified) before God. We always recognize that even this faith which justifies us is a gift of God. It is not something that we contributed ourselves. It is faith, but we have it because God gave it to us. "For by grace have you been saved through faith; and that not of yourselves, it is the gift of God, not as a result of works, that no one should boast" (Ephesians 2:8).

Second Conclusion

Thus, you see, believing the gospel is indeed trusting in Christ, but trusting in Christ with a trust that he gave to us, because we were unable to trust in him without his grace. We were unable to do anything. Because we realized that we were unable to do anything, we fled to Christ crying out for his mercy and forgiveness. The Bible tells us that he is ready and willing to receive us and forgive us of all our sins. He is ready to put a new heart within us that makes us want to love and follow after him. This is the essence of the gospel. This is what the experience of every believer looks like. If we trust in Christ we are Christians. Yet, it is not so much that faith saves us as it is that grace saves us. Even more so, it is not so much that grace saves us, as it is that Christ saves us. Jesus saves, and Jesus alone saves!

An Illustration

I heard an explanation of this once that may help you focus on what I am trying to say. Once a man was asked as to the time when he was saved. He tried to prove his salvation by naming a date, time and place that he had decided for Jesus. This he thought was proof that he was indeed a child of God. Another man, with more insight into the real meaning of the gospel, answered that He was saved about two thousand years ago about twenty minutes outside of Jerusalem on a hill called Golgotha.[5] I hope you see the difference between these two separate gospels. One focuses upon the act of man, and the other focuses on the act of Christ. One focuses on the faith of the man, and the other on the work of Christ. One is a false gospel, and the other is the true gospel. Paul put it plainly in Galatians 6:14, where he says, "But God forbid that I should glory, save in the cross of our Lord Jesus Christ."

---

[5] Generally attributed to Lutheran Theologian John Warwick Montgomery.

John 3:16

In the light of how I have just described the gospel, John 3:16 really takes on a new meaning. It guarantees hope to all those who see themselves as Hell-bound sinners, so deep in a dark pit that there is no way out. It gives hope to a helpless man who flees to Christ as his only hope for forgiveness and deliverance. "For God so loved the world that He gave His only begotten Son, that whosoever believes in Him shall not perish, but have everlasting life." The critical word in this verse is not "believes," but the critical word is "Him." That is the difference between many modern spurious gospels and the true gospel of Jesus Christ. It is only Christ who can pull me out of this deep pit, cleanse my heart, and enable me to walk in his ways. The focus is upon Christ, not upon faith. Our faith must not be in faith, but in Christ. Having faith is not the gospel, but faith is only the means to appropriate the gospel. The gospel is defined as the promises of the grace and power of the living Christ who saves his people from their sins.

John 3:16 also tells us that whosoever believes in Christ as his only hope for salvation will not be rejected. If you believe in Jesus as the Savior you shall not perish, but you shall inherit eternal life. Regardless of what you have done, regardless of how you have lived, the offer of the gospel comes with no strings attached. The only qualification is that you believe that you are unqualified and then look to Christ. God has never rejected anyone who comes to him with such hope. We know when we come to Christ for his mercy that he shall receive us. The Bible says in John 6:37, "All that the Father gives to Me will come to Me, and the one who comes to Me, I will certainly not cast out."

It is by grace alone through faith alone that Jesus alone saves. This is our only hope. Nothing else will save you, but this gospel will genuinely save you. Flee to Christ and call out for his mercy and power. His perfect life is a substitute for our failures. His death on a cross is a substitution for the penalty we deserve. Christ will save you to the uttermost.

As we look at our children, we want them to experience this attitude toward themselves and toward God. Even as they are raised in good homes, we still need to see them experience hopelessness in their own goodness and the joy of forgiveness. We want them to follow Christ and love his church just as we do. This is the hope of every Christian parent for their children. How the children come to understand and believe this is not as important as the fact that they do understand and believe it. People come to understand the gospel through various experiences. The experience that brings Christians to understand and believe the gospel is called conversion.

The main point here to remember is that even though the gospel is the same for all Christians, the way in which Christians come to believe in the gospel varies greatly. Children in the church certainly may have a different experience than a person like John Newton, who was a wicked slave trader before he was converted. You cannot and should not judge the reality of your own conversion by the testimony of another's conversion. This has caused deep hurt in the church. I will cover issues like this in my next chapter where I deal with the issue of conversion itself.

2

DEFINING SOME IMPORTANT WORDS

Introduction

In chapter one we looked at the meaning of the gospel. The gospel (the good news) is that as I come to understand that I am a sinner and that I am hopeless; and as I flee to Christ for forgiveness and the power to change my life, then God is willing and able to forgive me and change me. He will charge to my account the righteousness of Christ, and he will change me because He cannot deny his promises to anyone who comes to him. Christ receives all who come to him. He has never rejected anyone. Our hope is not in how good we are or even in how much faith we have. Our hope is in the power of Christ to save us from our sins and from the judgment to come.

As I mentioned in the previous chapter, Christians come to understand and believe the gospel in various ways. One thing that all Christians have in common is the same hope in the same Christ. However, Christians have different experiences as they travel this road of coming to believe the gospel. The testimony of how we came to believe and trust in Christ will vary from Christian to Christian. However, let me remind you again, that the important point is not how you got there but that you are there. We may be delivered from a major flood in various ways. Some escape by boat. Some escape by helicopter. Some are just able to quietly walk to a high spot before the water rises. Yet, the important point is not how dramatic or non-dramatic our escape was. We may compare stories about our escape. Some have spectacular stories and some not so remarkable, but the important point is that we are all safe.

Let's Define Some Terms First

Before I move on to the other chapters in this book, I believe it is important to define some terms. We often assume that we all have the same understanding of certain words, but I'm not so sure this is true. In order for the reader to understand better what I am saying about children and the church, I think it is important first to define some important terms.

"Regeneration"

In theological circles the terms regeneration and conversion are defined differently. Regeneration is the description of what God does in changing the heart of a man before he can believe the gospel. You are passive in your regeneration. God has to do this work. You can do nothing.

The terms "new birth" and "regeneration" are basically synonymous. They are two separate phrases for the same event in the life of a Christian. The necessity of being born again is almost a mantra in evangelical circles. You see it on billboards and road signs of all types.

The word "regeneration" is made up of two parts. One part is the word "generation." To generate means to produce life. The Book of Genesis gives us a description of how life began. The prefix "re" means "again." Thus the word regeneration means to be born a second time or again. This terminology comes from a statement that Jesus made to Nicodemus in John chapter 3.

Nicodemus was a religious leader (a Pharisee) among the Jews. He was what we might today call a theologian. In a conversation with Christ, he did not recognize that Christ was the coming Savior as was promised in the Old Testament. Nicodemus was a teacher but he did not understand the central point of what he was teaching. He recognized Christ as a great man because of the miracles and signs Christ had performed. He should have recognized Christ as the Son of God and the Savior of the world. He should have trusted in Christ as his only hope for salvation. He should have understood that before a man can come to Christ, there must be a supernatural work of God in the heart of the man. Jesus asked Nicodemus, "Are you the teacher of Israel and do not understand these things?" (John 3:10).

Jesus was very straight-forward with Nicodemus and in essence told him that he was not regenerated. He needed to be changed by the Spirit of God to understand the gospel. This is when Jesus told him that he needed to be born again. "Jesus answered and said to him, 'Truly, truly, I say to you, unless one is born again he cannot see the kingdom of God'" (John 3:3). Literally, the language is "born from above" but since Nicodemus responded by a reference to the natural birth of a child, the text has been translated as born again.

In the same way as a child comes out of the womb and sees the world in a new way for the first time, the adult Nicodemus needed to be changed inside so that he would have a new heart and a new mind. He needed to be brought from darkness into light. He needed to see everything differently. It is implied from a later text in the Gospel of John that Nicodemus was eventually born again because we are told in the Bible that he came to help with the burial of Jesus (John 19:39).

However, not all the New Testament saints had the same experience as Nicodemus. It appears that John the Baptist was regenerated in the womb of his mother. The mother of John the Baptist visited Mary the mother of Jesus while both babies were still in the womb. It appears that John the Baptist even in the womb rejoiced when he was in the presence of Jesus. I think it is safe to assume that this says something about the status and capability of children in the womb! This validates that a child in the womb is an actual person and not just a "fetus" that can be aborted. "When Elizabeth heard Mary's greeting, the baby leaped in her womb; and Elizabeth was filled with the Holy Spirit" (Luke 1:41). Now Elizabeth interpreted this event as follows: "For behold, when the sound of your greeting reached my ears, the baby leaped in my womb for joy" (Luke 1:44). John the Baptist leaped for joy in the womb when he was in the presence of Christ.

I believe that John the Baptist had been regenerated at this point. Although Jesus told Nicodemus that he needed to be born again, Jesus never told John the Baptist that he needed to be born again. He was already born again when he met Jesus as an adult. Even Jeremiah was known (loved) in the womb by God (Jer.1:5).

My point is simply that adult unbelievers like Nicodemus do need to be born again, but John the Baptist as an adult did not need to be born again. He had already been regenerated in his mother's womb. I would venture to say that some children today are born again in their mother's womb. Some children are regenerated outside of the womb as they are taught about Christ in the home and in the church. And then some children are not regenerated until they become adults.

All children in the church at some point need to publicly profess faith in Christ but to think of that particular time as the time of their new birth is improper. Some Christians are born again (regenerated) long before they make a public profession of faith as was John the Baptist, and on the other hand, some children are born again long after they are born into this world or even long after they make a profession of faith.

Often, in covenant children a profession of faith is just the outworking of their regeneration that may have occurred many years before — even back to the time they were in the womb. Then too, sometimes a public profession of faith may actually precede regeneration which may happen years later when the children actually experience hopelessness as an adult and then flee to Christ.

"Conversion"

The word conversion describes the experience that Christians have after they have been regenerated. Sometimes regeneration is so close in time to the attendant conversion experience that they may be viewed as occurring simultaneously. Yet, this must not negate the fact that regeneration is necessarily prior to the experience of faith in Christ. Christians are not active in their own regeneration or new birth. However, every Christian is active in his own conversion.

This term "conversion" describes the process of coming to faith and repentance in the life of the Christian. Conversion is turning directions. It is moving from a love of the world to a love of God. All Christians must have faith. They must see themselves as sinners and hopeless. They must believe and hope in Christ. They must see sin as offensive to God and seek God for forgiveness and for the power to turn from their sins.

This repentance and faith may come to different Christians at various times and in many ways. With some it comes in an instant. With others it comes over a long period of time after a considerable struggle. It's a little like the development of a child. All children must be born, and they are passive in that birth — not being able to choose the time, place, and date of their birth. However, following birth the experiences of growing into adulthood will vary greatly. Some are raised in America and some are raised in Africa. Some grow to be five feet tall, and some grow to be well over six feet tall. Some struggle with chronic illness and others are perfectly healthy. A child is not active in his or her own birth, but every child is very active in the experience of arriving at adulthood. Likewise, a Christian is passive in regard to choosing the time and place of his birth (regeneration), yet like a child, every Christian will be active in their own conversion. They must exercise faith and repentance. They must experience hopelessness and consequently a hope in Christ.

Thus, it is important to distinguish between regeneration and conversion. They describe two different events in the life of the Christian. One (regeneration) describes the passive work that God does in the heart of a person while the other (conversion) describes the active experience that people have as they turn from hope in themselves to hope in Christ.

"Election"

This is not a book dealing with all the various doctrines of the Christian faith in great detail. Numerous books have been written on these various topics. However, in order to understand the issue of the covenant and our children, we must have at least a minimal level of understanding of the various terms that are used in the Bible including the doctrine of election.

Remember that regeneration is totally a work of God without any cooperation with man. God alone regenerates. One of the questions that arises when we discuss regeneration and conversion is why does God choose to regenerate some and not others. If regeneration originates from God, and Christians are passive in their own new birth, then it must follow that God alone is the author of regeneration. How then do you explain the assumption that God chooses to regenerate only some?

The most popular answer to this dilemma is that God chooses certain people because he saw ahead of time that they would believe in Christ of their own free-will. After he saw ahead that the unregenerate would believe, then he elected that person. Then God regenerated their hearts so that they would believe. Or even worse, they believed and then God regenerated their hearts. In the view of some, regeneration follows a decision of the will. However, this answer to the dilemma removes the ultimate decision of salvation from God and puts it in the will of man. This ultimately reduces the source of election in salvation to a choice that man makes. God only reacts to man's choice as God sees this free-will choice of man before the foundation of the world. This is the way that some people handle the doctrine of election. This is quite contrary to the teaching of the Bible.

What then is the answer to this dilemma? Why then does God choose to regenerate some and not others? It is quite obvious that not everyone believes when they hear the gospel. If the Bible teaches that man cannot regenerate himself or that election is not merely something God did because he foresaw what man first would do, then how can we get ourselves out of this mess? Indeed it does seem like a mess! It seems to be rather unfair on God's part. This is an old problem that has plagued the church for centuries. I will attempt to answer this question below.

How is it fair that God chooses to regenerate some and not others? The Bible itself explains how we are to respond to this question. The bottom line is that the reason for God's election is mysterious. It is unexplainable. It is something we do not understand and must leave with God. It's a little like the doctrine of the Trinity. It is inexplicable. However, just because we cannot understand why God elects only some does not mean that we must deny that he does elect only some.

God is not limited by our understanding. What we do know for certain is that he does it for his own glory. If man contributes anything to his own salvation, then it takes away from God's glory and the glories of his grace. Even the faith we exercise is a gift of God. The Bible clearly teaches us to approach this dilemma in this way, leaving it shrouded in mystery, but maintaining that all glory belongs to God.

Actually, no matter in which direction we go, there is a dilemma. The suggestion that God chooses ahead those who he foresaw would believe leaves us with a dilemma. Man ultimately is the source of his own salvation. On the other hand, if God chooses who will be born again apart from relying on the foresight of man's decision, then this leaves us with a dilemma. God appears to be unfair.

Paul, who understood the difficulty of this quandary, anticipated this latter objection as he examined this issue in Romans 9. Just the fact that he anticipated the latter objection of unfairness on God's part is evidence that we are asking the right question. Paul too asked the same question. In Romans 9:14 Paul says, "What shall we say then? There is no injustice with God, is there? May it never be!" Paul goes on to teach that God is not unfair. God forbid! How could God be unfair? If he were unfair, he could not be God.

Thus, the answer to this dilemma is simply that although it is true that God predestines some for regeneration before the foundation of the world (Eph. 1:4), we cannot understand it fully.

One thing we do know for sure — God is fair! This is a mystery we must leave with God.

This does not mean that men who choose not to believe in Christ are off the hook. The Bible teaches clearly that if anyone rejects the gospel or does not believe the gospel, then that person is personally responsible for his choice. If he rejects Christ then God will hold him guilty for rejecting his Son. Rejection of Christ is a personal sin against God, and God will not hold him guiltless. This is a great mystery too. How can a man be *unable* to believe and yet be *responsible* to believe? It all boils down to this. I personally don't understand it, but I have learned to accept it. When there is salvation, God gets all the glory, and when there is rejection of God, man gets all the blame. That is where I learned to leave it all. For an excellent explanation of this view see J. I. Packer's book on *Evangelism and the Sovereignty of God.*[6]

I have heard many humble saints who believe in election say that the great mystery to them is that God would choose to save any at all, especially them. None of us deserve to be saved. We all deserve condemnation. That God would save anyone is the real anomaly!

Again, God is sovereign and we must leave the mystery with him. It is not a question that we are even worthy to ask. "On the contrary, who are you, O man, who answers back to God? The thing molded will not say to the molder, 'Why did you make me like this,' will it? Or does not the potter have a right over the clay, to make from the same lump one vessel for honorable use and another for common use" (Rom. 9:20–21). Hey, it is a mystery to me, but God tells me to leave it there.

It is a predicament no matter which way you go. The difference between the two views is that one sees man as partly contributing to his salvation, and the other gives God all the glory for his salva-

---

[6] J. I. Packer, *Evangelism and the Sovereignty of God* (Downers Grove, Ill: IVP Academic, 1991).

tion (Eph. 1:6). The Bible clearly identifies with the latter solution to the dilemma.

Indeed, this is a complicated issue. I believe it is biblical that regeneration is a work of God in which we are passive, and conversion is also a work of God where we are active in believing in Christ with a faith given to us by the grace of God. The only reason we believe and trust in the Savior is because God chose us in Christ before the foundation of the world (Eph. 1). He did not choose us because we were better than anyone else. We were as bad or had the potential to be as bad as anyone else. He chose us to demonstrate his own mercy. He decided to have mercy on some, and we are thankful that he had mercy on us.

The fact that God chose to have mercy on you should only make you proclaim how amazing his grace really is. You certainly can't brag about how you decided to follow Jesus. You can only bow in humility that God would have grace on you and not pass you by. Don't try to reason it all out. Just take the good parts (such as it gives all glory to God and you are saved totally by grace), and then leave the rest (what seems to be unfair) to the mind of God.

There is one more benefit from the doctrine of election (predestination) that sometimes is overlooked. Paul alludes to it in Philippians 1:6: "For I am confident of this very thing, that He who began a good work in you will perfect it until the day of Christ Jesus." Because God began the work of salvation in us, we know he will keep that faith in us until we die. He will not let us go. Our hope for persevering in the faith is not in our own ability to keep the faith, but rather it is in God's ability to keep us in the faith. This he promises to do, and we can take great comfort in his faithfulness.

If this still bothers you, then probably you do not understand how to handle it just as was the case with me years ago. Before I go on, let me just remind you of what Jesus taught in John 3:16. "For God so loved the world that He gave His only begotten Son, that whoever believes in Him shall not perish, but have eternal life." Regardless of who you are or what you have done, the gospel message is for you. Whosoever believes in Christ shall be saved.

Take great comfort in this as I had to do when I first heard the doctrine of election (sometimes called the doctrine of predestination). I was floored by it!

God will not reject anyone who comes to Christ. However, after you come to Christ, you should understand that the only reason you came to Christ was because God chose to regenerate you and give you the ability to exercise faith in Christ. God predestined you as his elect before the world began (Eph 1:1–6). This is why we call these views the doctrines of grace. Ultimately, I can contribute nothing to my own salvation. Yes, I must believe and turn to Christ but even the ability to believe is a gift of God because he chose to regenerate me. Faith is the ultimate evidence of election. "For by grace have you been saved through faith; and that not of yourselves, it is a gift of God" (Eph. 2:8). Christians "were born, not of blood, nor of the will of the flesh, nor of the will of man, but of God" (John 1:13).

The reason I included an overview of election in this chapter is because it does affect how we view our children. Since God does make promises in the covenant to our children about their salvation, it gives us hope for them. As we are responsible in raising our children up in the fear and admonition of the Lord, we have hope that God will regenerate their hearts. We have hope that we will see the same faith in them that we see in ourselves. Our hope is not in the power of our children to choose God or even in ourselves to help them choose God, but rather in the power of God to choose our children.

Honestly, as I look at children, I don't see much hope in their own hearts. However, there is hope in Christ. Praise God! This does not nullify the work that we need to do in raising our children as I will explain in Chapter 6 of this book, but it only sets before us the importance of that work as we trust in the promises of God.

"Salvation"

The word "salvation" describes the entire process of the work of God as he works in the life of a Christian. It covers the entire span of the work of God from our election to our regeneration to our conversion — and even to our glorification. Glorification is being taken up into heaven and ultimately being reunited with our bodies at the final resurrection. The word salvation can be applied to one part of this process as well as to the whole process from beginning to end. It is interesting that the Bible uses the word salvation (or other forms of it) in three different tenses. We have been saved, we are being saved, and we shall be saved. Notice the various tenses used in the following three passages from the Bible.

> "For by grace you *have been saved* [italics mine] through faith; and that not of yourselves, it is the gift of God" (Eph. 2:8).

> "For the word of the cross is foolishness to those who are perishing, but to us who *are being saved* [italics mine] it is the power of God" (I Cor. 1:18).

> "Much more then, having now been justified by His blood, we *shall be saved* [italics mine] from the wrath of God through Him" (Rom. 5:9)

The word "salvation" is often interchanged with the word "justify," but this is a mistake. Justification is a legal term that describes an act of God that occurs in an instant. Salvation includes justification, but it also includes much more. Salvation, as it includes the various phases of being saved, is progressive. It includes justification, adoption, sanctification, and glorification. It is a lifelong process.

Often people say that they were saved at a particular time, not realizing that the word "salvation" describes the whole process of salvation from election to glorification. The Apostle Paul alludes to this in the Book of Philippians where he says, "So then, my beloved, just as you have always obeyed, not as in my presence only, but now much more in my absence, work out your own salvation with fear and trembling; for it is God who is at work in you, both to will and to work for *His* good pleasure" (Phil 2:12–13).

"Sanctification"

I won't spend much time on the word sanctification since there is not much disagreement in the church about it. Sanctification is the description of the work of God in the life of a Christian after he becomes a Christian. Sanctification describes the struggle of growing in grace and knowledge in Christ. Regeneration is instantaneous. Like salvation which describes a process (and includes sanctification), sanctification is progressive. It is a life-time journey. It is full of ups and downs, but in the long-term, Christians should make progress with their struggle against sin. They will not be fully sanctified (made perfect) until they are in heaven with Christ.

Conclusion

My goal in this chapter has been to define some common words that are used among Christians. Hopefully, now you have some working definitions of important terms that are used in the Bible. In the following chapters we shall put these terms to use especially as we consider children raised in the church. In the next chapter of this book I will give a testimony of my own experience before we look at various conversion experiences recorded in the Bible. Before I understood the meaning of some of these basic terms, as you will see, my life was a testimony of much confusion.

THE NATURE OF CONVERSION EXAMINED

My Own Experience

Now, I hope the definitions in the previous chapter have been helpful. It is important that we distinguish between regeneration and conversion. When a Christian describes his experience of coming to Christ, he is describing his conversion. He is not describing his regeneration. Let me state clearly again the meaning of the word conversion.

Conversion describes the transition we have as we come to understand our hopeless condition and trust in Christ. Before we look at several conversion experiences in the Bible, let me first give a short description of my own experience. In so many ways, I believe my experience is typical of numerous Christians in the church, especially those who were raised in the church from the time they were small children.

When I was a young child my mother decided that she was going to take me and my siblings to church. She and my father had five children. My mother had a very difficult childhood, and she did not want her children to experience the difficult life that she had to endure as a child. I believe this was her motive for going to church. From somewhere in her past she learned that there was hope in the church. Maybe there was an ancestor who was a Christian who prayed for her. She loved her children, and in her mind the church might provide them a hope which she did not know as a child. The church might save her children from having to go through the same hard times she had to endure. My mother chose the nearest church which, as it happened, was visible from our house. It was a small white clapboard Presbyterian Church in the mountains of West Virginia that probably would seat a total of about fifty people.

My father did not make a profession of faith in Christ until later in life after a bad automobile accident that nearly took the lives of several members of my family. As a young person there was not much Christianity in our home, but there was, as was common for that generation, a high regard for Christian morality. As most parents were then, my mother and father were rather reserved and private.

From the time I was a child the Bible had a great impact on me. The Bible was always God's holy word to me. I cannot remember a time when I did not believe this. No doubt, the church led me to believe this. I always had the greatest respect for the men who pastored our little church even though I knew they had flaws in their own lives. I was constantly in both Sunday School and church hearing the Bible taught and preached. I believed whatever was taught from the Bible. I never questioned the teachings of the Bible.

As I grew into my teenage years, I began to doubt the genuineness of my own faith. I wondered if I were even a Christian. I had heard about others having major, dramatic conversions. I did not have a dramatic conversion; therefore, I did not have a remarkable testimony about how I came to Christ. To the extent that I understood conversion at that time, I believed that I did not have a conversion experience; so how could I be a Christian? I was very bashful and I never did walk forward in a revival meeting. I did however make a profession of faith once in our little church and then was baptized.

Even after that, I still did not feel converted. I suppose one problem I had was that I was not sure how a converted person was supposed to feel. I based everything on how I felt. I would understand the problem with this later, but for the time being, I was totally confused. I asked my pastor to baptize me again, and he did. I still did not feel any better about my own conversion. I suppose I could have asked my pastor to baptize me a third time, and he probably would have done it; but I began to realize that being baptized another time just was not going to give me the feeling of being the Christian that I thought I needed to be.

I lived a very moral life, believed in the Bible, and knew that I had to trust in Christ for the forgiveness of my sins. I never doubted the power of God to forgive sins because of the work of Christ on the cross. Jesus was the Son of God as well as the Son of Man. However, this just did not seem to be enough! In my own mind I needed some dramatic experience. I had no time, date, and place where I could say that I had become a Christian. I had no emotional experience that I could call my conversion. I had a date, time, and place when I had been baptized. Actually I had two of those, but baptism from my view at the time, just did not do the job.

Off to a state college I went as a professing Christian who had been raised in the church. I lived at home and commuted back and forth daily to school. Living at home probably helped keep me out of a lot of mischief and sin.

I did well in college. I majored in mathematics and was offered a graduate teaching-assistantship at West Virginia University. I always wanted to teach, and I had the goal of teaching mathematics on a college level. However, my spirit was troubled. I had come to believe that maybe I needed to give my life "full-time" to Christian service. At the time, being a minister in the church was the only way I knew how to do that. Too, I thought maybe this would give me assurance that I was a Christian. This would bring closure to my struggles with my faith. So I thought!

There ensued a tension in my life between going on to graduate school to study mathematics and going to seminary to prepare for the ministry. I loved learning. I loved mathematics but I thought the only way to truly serve God was going into the gospel ministry. Thus my spirit was greatly torn within me. I ended up in the hospital with a bleeding colon just before my graduation from college. My grandmother died of colon cancer, and my poor mother was fraught with fear for me. My mother was not aware of the spiritual struggles going on inside of me. Like many young people I was afraid (and ashamed) to share my inner thoughts with other people. I thought maybe God was judging me for being too worldly and seeking a career in mathematics. Maybe I was rejecting God?

Later I would learn differently, but there was to be a long wait before I better understood these things.

While in college, I remember one professor who enjoyed challenging Christians in class. He identified with Karl Marx and taught that Christianity was the "opiate of the masses." He believed that his responsibility was not only to teach economics but to lead young misguided students out of the bondage of Christianity. I remember being afraid to argue with him in class. Don't forget that I was very timid and backward. This added to my guilt. I did not speak up for Christ. Maybe I was ashamed of Christ? I certainly was afraid of the professor. I knew I could not go toe to toe with him in a debate.

So, to the disappointment of my parents, who were so proud of their son who had received a teaching-assistantship at the state university, I went off to seminary at Westminster Theological Seminary in Philadelphia, Pennsylvania. Probably, guilt and doubt were the emotions that were leading me there. No doubt, seminary changed my life. My church at home was a blue-collar church. From my experience in college when compared with my experience in my own church, it seemed to me that educated people who had doctorate degrees did not believe in the Bible.

Well, at Westminster Seminary I experienced just the opposite. There were professors everywhere with a Ph.D. or a Th. D. behind their names who believed in the authority of the Bible. Also, in seminary I was confronted with the doctrine of predestination. At that time, because I did not really understand the doctrine, this further diminished what assurance I had. If God elected before the foundation of the world who was to be saved and who was not to be saved, then maybe I was not among the elect? Again, later on I was able to deal with this dilemma.

To make a long story short, from there I was off to being ordained into the ministry and began a long run at being a pastor for some forty years. I must confess that even as a minister, I sometimes had this nagging thought in the back of my mind that maybe I was not really converted because I never had a dramatic experience. I usually brushed that off by just quoting to myself John 3:16.

However, somewhere along the line the truth hit me. I did not need a dramatic conversion experience. Some Christians had such an experience and others did not. Eventually I came to understand that my assurance should not be based upon my experience or upon how I felt. It should not be based upon how much faith I had. It should not even be based upon all the work I had done as a preacher. As I mentioned in the previous chapter, belief in Christ is not a faith that trusts in how much faith a Christian has. It is not faith in faith. It is a faith that comes to understand that my only hope in this life and the life to come is in the person of Jesus Christ. I needed to look outwardly to Christ and not look inwardly at what was inside of me. Looking inwardly only depressed me. Looking outwardly to Christ gave me a final resting place.

I now see that this slow process from childhood to adulthood was my conversion experience. It took me a long time to totally rest in Christ, but through all of this I came to see that I was looking in the wrong places for assurance. I believe that I was a Christian as a child, but I now believe that my problem then was the issue of the assurance of my salvation. I needed to look to Christ alone. This is one reason I have written this book. Even though we all come to Christ in different ways and along different paths — that is not the important thing. Being in a state where I know that Christ is my only hope is the important thing. It's not so important how you escaped from the flood waters. What is important is that you are safe.

My thesis in this book is that not everyone has the same conversion experience. Some do indeed have dramatic experiences. John Newton, a former slave-trader, was converted and later wrote the hymn "Amazing Grace." He was blind spiritually, and then he was able to see. That was his testimony as an adult. I was never blind that I can remember. I was confused, but not blind. I was not a slave-trader. I was a nice boy from West Virginia who believed in the Bible from the time I was a child. All I needed was to understand the nature of true faith. I finally did. Faith focuses on Christ and not on me. Christ is my only resting place.

Along the way, during my conversion, I realized that I needed to support my views from the Bible itself. Not every Christian has the same conversion experience, but every Christian should have the same basic faith. Is this taught in the Bible? Indeed it is. Let's take a look at this now.

Conversion Experiences in the Bible

I do believe that the Bible is the word of God. As I mentioned previously, I was convinced of this from the time I was a child. The Bible gives numerous examples of how various people came to believe in Christ. I have spent a great amount of time looking at the various conversion experiences in the Scriptures, and finally I came to some concrete conclusions about the nature of conversion. There are various types of conversions in the Bible. Some are dramatic and instantaneous. Some are not dramatic at all. Some Christians could give a date, time, and place, and I believe others could not. The following sections will give some examples of both dramatic and non-dramatic conversions in the Bible.

The Apostle Paul – A Dramatic Conversion

There may not be any more dramatic conversion in the Bible than that of the Apostle Paul. Paul describes his life before he was a Christian (in Philippians 3:6) as being "a persecutor of the church." He also mentions in 1 Timothy 1:13 that he was a blasphemer where he said, "even though I was formerly a blasphemer and a persecutor and a violent aggressor" he was shown mercy by God.

Paul's conversion was initiated by a direct and audible confrontation with Christ himself. We are told in Acts 9:3-4 that "as he was traveling, it happened that he was approaching Damascus, and suddenly a light from heaven flashed around him; and he fell to the ground and heard a voice saying to him, 'Saul, Saul, why are you persecuting Me?'" Saul (whose name was later changed to Paul) was totally confused. He was now literally blind. "Saul got up from the ground, and though his eyes were open, he could see nothing; and leading him by the hand, they brought him into Damascus" (Acts 9:8).

Paul's blindness was healed in Damascus through the ministry of a man named Ananias doing what God told him to do. Then the Bible tells us that "immediately there fell from his eyes something like scales, and he regained his sight, and he got up and was baptized; and he took food and was strengthened" (Acts 9:18–19). After spending several days with some of Christ's disciples, Paul began to preach about Christ.

No doubt Paul could give a date, a time, and a place of his conversion. The change in him was dramatic – from a hater of Christ to a preacher of Christ in just a few days. Let me say that Paul's conversion experience was unique. You should not expect the same type of experience in your life. A few others have claimed something similar, like Joseph Smith who founded the Mormon Cult, but such experiences are bogus. Paul was miraculously called audibly by God to be the "Apostle to the Gentiles," and we should not seek to duplicate his experience. There are many other conversions in the Bible. Some are dramatic and some are not, but Paul's was unique.

Some Other Conversions

On the day of Pentecost there is a record of about three thousand souls being converted on that day after the sermon was finished. After hearing Peter preach about Christ and after being accused of putting Christ to death, these Jews asked Peter, "Brethren, what must we do?" (Acts 2:37). Peter said to them, "Repent and each of you be baptized for the forgiveness of sins; and you will receive the gift of the Holy Spirit" (Acts 2:38).

Thus, each of these Jews saw their guilt and hopelessness and turned to Christ for the forgiveness of their sins, many having participated in the murder of Christ. They were baptized which was an outward sign and seal from God that their sins were forgiven. Later we will look at the concept of a sign and seal in baptism. The point here is that they experienced conversion. It is likely that their regeneration happened on that same day. They could name a date, a time, and a place of their conversion.

Later on in Acts 3, Peter preached a second sermon and more people were converted. The total of those converted at that point in time was about five thousand people. They too were immediately transformed in their thinking and became followers of Christ. They changed directions. They could name a date, a time, and a place.

The Book of Acts is full of similar accounts. In Acts 16:14, Lydia instantly responded to the things spoken by Paul. In Acts 16:33 the Philippian jailor was converted dramatically in the middle of the night. Both could name a date, a time, and a place.

Now, obviously many other illustrations could be given, especially from the testimonies in the Four Gospels. My point in this chapter is not to doubt the reality of the testimony of many Christians who were dramatically changed in an instant. No doubt, history is full of stories of such dramatic conversions. I need not spend any more time on this. However, one of my points in this book is to demonstrate that many Christians do not have such dramatic conversions, but they have been converted nonetheless.

The Book of Acts is the story of the beginning of the New Testament Church. The gospel of the good news about the death and resurrection of Christ was new. It was being presented to a generation that was in rebellion against God and who, unlike our own day and time, had never heard the gospel. We would therefore expect such dramatic accounts.

Timothy – No Dramatic Conversion Experience

Yet, there are accounts in the Bible of Christians who give no evidence of a date, a time, and a place of when they became a Christian. If they did have a date, a time, and a place, they felt no need to mention it. There is no dramatic experience that was recorded. As far as we know there was no walking down the aisle or praying the sinner's prayer.

One example of such a person is Timothy. What do we know about Timothy? Paul wrote two letters to Timothy that make up two books of the Bible. Timothy was an evangelist and a pastor. As we search the Scriptures, we gain a great deal of knowledge about the life of Timothy. Timothy was one of those covenant children like me who believed in the Bible (in his day the Bible was the Old Testament) from the time he was a child. Paul wrote to Timothy and said, "You, however, continue in the things you have learned and become convinced of, knowing from whom you have learned them, and that from childhood you have known the sacred writings which are able to give you the wisdom that leads to salvation through faith which is in Christ Jesus" (2 Timothy 3:14–15). Timothy was a covenant child raised in a godly home and it would have been expected that he would believe that Christ was the Savior.

Paul also says in 2 Timothy 1:5, "For I am mindful of the sincere faith within you, which first dwelt in your grandmother Lois and your mother Eunice, and I am sure that it is in you as well." This is a mystery, but in some sense, Paul was convinced that the same saving faith that was in his mother and grandmother was in Timothy as well. Timothy's faith could be attributed to his family. He was raised by a godly mother and grandmother and from this upbringing there resulted saving faith in Timothy. We must not ignore this.

It has been my privilege to know many godly men in the ministry who are now with the Lord in heaven. It has also been my privilege to know their children as adults who now have their own children. How often I see the faith of the father (and mother) in the children! The adult children are images of their parents, not only physically but spiritually.

Even greater, how often I see the faith of the father in his grand-children. Godliness gives birth to godliness unto many generations. To see it actually brings tears of joy to my eyes. It is a joy to see grandchildren who physically display the characteristics of both their parents and grandparents, but it is even a greater joy to see the same zeal for Christ and the same fruit of the Spirit in the offspring. The faith of the fathers do indeed dwell in their children.

There is nothing in the Scriptures about Timothy having a dramatic conversion. There is only evidence to the contrary. What we do have is a man who believed in Christ, and his faith can be attributed to how he was raised. He was raised in a home where the Bible was upheld with all respect and reverence, and the faith of his family had been transferred to him. His mother and grandmother were models of godliness. Although Timothy had to believe in Christ at some point and be baptized, he had been prepared for this from his childhood. I doubt that Timothy had any particular "road to Damascus" experience. He simply believed the Bible from the time he was a child. He believed that Jesus was the promised Messiah. This is what we should expect of most children raised in the church. No dramatic experience. No remarkable testimony.

Other examples of believers without a dramatic conversion experience include Elizabeth, the mother of John the Baptist, and her husband Zacharias. The Bible simply makes the following statement about both of them. "They were both righteous in the sight of God, walking blamelessly in all the commandments and requirements of the Lord" (Luke 1:6). Nothing dramatic here — just a statement of the facts!

As I alluded to before, the same can be said of their son, John the Baptist. The description of John is given to us in Luke 1:15. "For he will be great in the sight of the Lord; and he will drink no wine or liquor, and he will be filled with the Holy Spirit while yet in his mother's womb." There was no dramatic conversion experience in John's life. He came out of the womb regenerated, and just like Timothy, he also had the benefit of being raised by godly parents.

A Qualification

Now, don't get me wrong. Not everyone raised in the church or even in a godly family will have such faith at an early age. Some do drift away and have to be called back to the fold. Oftentimes, such covenant children do have dramatic stories. Some covenant children seem to live in another world and never give much thought to the nature of their faith. Some of them stray far away from the church and live like pagans. Some continue to be a part of the church and live like pagans! Some leaders of the church just write it off as a time when there is the need to sow wild seeds.

I have heard older Christians seeking to justify this by saying: "It's what young men do, but it won't last long." Some of these children later may have a dramatic experience of conversion. However, my point is that this is not the case with all covenant children. Again, my conclusion is that God calls us in various ways as we walk various pathways. Some, like me, cannot remember any particular time that we were converted. I have always believed in Christ, and that should be enough.

One of the dangers of having a dramatic conversion experience is to demand the same of others. There can be a tendency of some Christians to condescend to others who lack the same experience as they have had. In some churches there almost seems to be competition in regard to who has the most dramatic testimony about their conversion experience. Being delivered out of witchcraft is much more interesting than sitting at the feet of a mother for years and slowly coming to faith in Christ.

When I was in Seminary, I remember another student who used to look at me as if I were not a Christian because I did not have a dramatic conversion experience. He viewed me as an unconverted young man who was raised in church, and since I never had a conversion experience like his, therefore I could not be a Christian. I know he was sincere, but now looking back upon it, I believe it was only a spirit of arrogance on his part.

The Problem with Early New England Puritans

This was a problem with the early New England Puritans after they came to America. When these godly people came to America, they experienced a great deal of trial and difficulty. From the raging seas of crossing the Atlantic to the threat of Indians, they had learned experimentally to lean upon Christ. They were constantly faced with death and disease. Contrary to their parents, their children and grandchildren were raised with the benefits attained by the sacrifices of their fathers. Their descendents enjoyed a more peaceful upbringing without all the difficulties that their parents experienced. Thus they had no dramatic stories to tell. Most of them were simply baptized and trusted in Christ as they grew older. They sought to live a moral life because it was a testimony to the goodness of Christ. But this was not good enough for their Puritan fathers. Their children could not give a testimony of an "on the road to Damascus" experience.

Thus, many of the early Puritans did not consider their own children as being converted. Even though their children had been baptized as infants, their children were not allowed to become full members of the local church because they could not give to their elders a testimony of some experience that demonstrated a dramatic conversion. They had been baptized into the church, but they were not allowed to take the Lord's Supper. This created even more problems when their children had their own children.

Since the Puritans did not consider their own children as being converted, then the question arose if they should administer baptism to their grandchildren? To administer baptism to their grandchildren would be administering baptism to the children of their own unconverted children. It would be tantamount to administering baptism to the children of the unconverted. This led to much controversy in the Puritan church[7], and sadly within a few generations the Puritans lost most of their children to the world. If only they had been more aware that conversion experiences do differ! If only they had not expected their children to duplicate their own conversion experiences. The Puritans meant well, but many of them lost their children. In my opinion, they drove their children away from the church. It is a sad story in American history.

---

[7]Robert G. Pope, *The Half-Way Covenant: Church Membership in Puritan New England* (Princeton: University Press, 1970).

Conclusion

In this chapter I have described the nature of my own conversion and demonstrated the conversion experiences of many of those in the early church. I have applied some of the definitions of the previous chapters to myself and to the life of other Christians. To summarize, remember that conversion is not the same thing as regeneration. Regeneration precedes faith. In regeneration you are passive. You cannot choose a date, time, and place of your regeneration. God regenerates by the total power of his own will and according to his own choice. The timing is his decision.

This causes a difficult problem because then we have to ask the question of why God chooses to regenerate some and not others. In order to deal with this dilemma, we looked at the doctrine of election in the previous chapter which is clearly taught in the Bible.

In this chapter I have concentrated on the issue of conversion. I demonstrated that even though all Christians must be born again, and all Christians must have the same type of faith in the same Christ; yet, the experience of how they come to faith will vary considerably from Christian to Christian. Some have dramatic conversion experiences and others do not. One of the problems I am dealing with in this book is the problem of the Puritans and a problem also I find that still exists in much of the church today. We cannot duplicate the conversion experience of others, and we should not try. Paul and Timothy had totally different conversion experiences. It should be expected that the conversion experience of those raised in the church will differ considerably from those converted as adults. In the next chapter we will give our attention to the idea of a covenant and how it affects the conversion of children in the church.

4

THE CONCEPT OF A COVENANT

Introduction

Now that we have defined our terms and looked at the concept of conversion, we are ready to look at how this applies to our children. To understand this we must understand the meaning of the term "covenant." What is a covenant? How does a covenant affect our understanding of the Scriptures? How does a covenant affect our understanding of the conversion of our children? In this and the following two chapters, I will attempt to answer these questions.

First, I think it is important to say that understanding the concept of a covenant is so important that it will affect how you read the Bible. It is that important! Once you understand the concept of a covenant, you may never read the Bible in the same way again. Let me explain.

We are predisposed to read the Bible in certain ways that often result from such things as the way we were raised, the church we attend, our conversion experience, or other things like our culture and even our ethnic background. In some sense, we all approach the Bible with a certain set of glasses over our eyes, and we tend to see things differently depending on the type of glasses we are wearing. If one person has on yellow-tinted glasses, he sees everything with a shade of yellow. If another person has on red-tinted glasses, he will see everything with a shade of red. Likewise, when we approach the Bible we do not come to it as neutral readers. We all have presuppositions and we tend to read those presuppositions into the texts of the Bible. Thus, coming to the Bible and knowing that the Bible is written in covenantal language will affect how we read it.

As an example of our predisposed bias in reading the Bible, if you believe God is sovereign, then you will see God as the one who ordains whatever comes to pass. However, if you believe that sovereignty is limited on the part of God, then you will view the God of the Bible as one who is trying to execute his will, but man by his own will is frustrating what God is attempting to do. These are two different views of God that affect how we read the Bible.

As another example, if you believe that the miraculous gifts in the Bible continue today, then you will view God as continuing to give those gifts to Christians in the modern age (speaking in tongues, faith-healing, etc.). If you believe those gifts were limited to New Testament times, then you will read the Bible differently. You will not be seeking those gifts.

Reading the Bible through the eye-glasses of the covenant enables us to see things quite differently. That is one reason why Presbyterians use the word covenant so much. It describes how they approach the Bible.

As I mentioned before, it is important to note that the word covenant is used in the Bible over 300 times. The idea of a covenant is not something that originates outside of the Bible, but rather it is at the very core of how the Bible speaks of itself. Actually, the Bible itself can be viewed as a covenant book.

I hold the view that the names "Old Testament" and "New Testament" should have been labeled the "Old Covenant" and "New Covenant." It should be understood that the title pages in your Bible that introduce the material of the Old Testament and the New Testament are not God-inspired. What we identify as the writings of the Old Testament and the New Testament are inspired (God-breathed), but the title pages that introduce them are not. They were added years after the Bible was completed in order to organize the Bible. The word "testament" is only used in the Bible 14 times in the King James Version (KJV). In the New American Standard Version (NASV) the word testament does not appear at all, except on the two title pages. Each Greek word translated as testament in the KJV is actually the word for covenant.

In translating the word covenant from the Greek into the Vulgate (Latin) version of the Bible, the early translator Jerome used the Latin word *testamentum* because there was no Latin equivalent of the word covenant. Thus, it became the common practice of all translators to use the word testament rather than the word covenant. Yes, it is my opinion that the two parts of the Bible should be labeled as the Old Covenant and the New Covenant, but I think it is too late to make that change now. I don't quite have that much influence in the world of Christendom.

Presbyterians use the word covenant a great deal. There is a college called Covenant College. There is a seminary called Covenant Seminary. Many church schools are called Covenant School. There are churches named Covenant Presbyterian Church all over America. One of the publishing houses in Reformed and Presbyterian circles is called Crown and Covenant Publications.

However, if you asked the average member of a Presbyterian Church what the word covenant means, you would probably only get a stare. Most likely they would not know. They might say it has something to do with children, but then they probably would say that they were not even sure of that. It is a sad fact that most Presbyterians do not understand the meaning of the concept of a covenant. I have read well-educated Presbyterian authors for years, and most often the concept of the covenant has been absent from their vocabulary — and I think from their theology. It discourages me when I find that many Presbyterian ministers do not think in terms of the covenant.

Yes, the covenant has something to do with children, but actually it deals with much more than that. I don't blame the member in the pew for his lack of knowledge, but I do think that the pastors and teachers in Presbyterian circles do bear some responsibility for this lack of understanding. Part of my purpose in writing this book is to help correct that deficiency.

Since the covenant does have a great deal to do with how we view our children, let me introduce this section by covering a few prominent views of the children of believers that exist in the modern church. I think this will help stimulate your curiosity in regard to how the covenant uniquely relates to our children.

Several Views of the Children of Christians

First, there is in the church a view that all children are born unregenerate, and that they can be regenerated by some rite administered by the church. This view holds that the administration of the rite of baptism to babies automatically regenerates them. I'm not sure what happens if the child dies before they are baptized. I would imagine there is some sort of exemption for this case.

This view is popular in the Roman Catholic Church. I would call it the sacramental view. Some would call it baptismal regeneration. Once the water is applied, the child is automatically regenerated in his heart. The work of God that regenerates them by the administration of baptism is *ex opere operato* which means in the Latin "from the work worked." The rite itself works regeneration into their hearts. Presbyterians do not believe this.

At the other extreme of the spectrum is another view quite common in the church today. It basically believes that all children are born going to heaven. However, if the children live to what is called the age of accountability, then they are viewed as lost, going to hell, and then they need to be saved. The goal of the church is to get them saved by leading them to make some type of profession of faith in Christ whenever they reach the age of accountability. The age of accountability appears to vary from child to child. The children may be urged to walk an aisle or they may be induced to bow their heads and pray the sinner's prayer. Some may just be asked to raise their hands if they want to go to heaven rather than hell. Regardless, there is an attempt to get the child to respond in some way.

Then, following this they will be baptized and encouraged never to doubt their salvation again. From my perspective of this view, it appears that in some sense these children are chronologically saved at birth, then lost somewhere between birth and the age of accountability, and then saved again when they walk the aisle or raise their hand in a Sunday School class. The age that children are encouraged to make some type of response may be very young.

It seems to me that few of these children really understand the nature of what they are doing. I think some response on the part of the child is more important for the parents (and other leaders in the church or school) than it is for the child. Every parent wants the assurance that their children will be saved. In my view, this method is actually something akin to infant baptism; it is just what I would call a delayed infant baptism. However, this perspective often assumes that regeneration is part and parcel with a profession of faith. As I mentioned before, in some circles it is even believed that the movement of the will is what triggers regeneration in the child. Again, refer to my definitions in Chapter 2. There I argue that regeneration precedes the actual act of the will in making a profession of faith in Christ.

Now, let's look at another view before we investigate the covenantal view. The view of the Westminster Standards is that all elect infants are going to heaven.[8] The only hope for some Calvinists (who believe that regeneration precedes faith) is that their children may be among the elect. They may be among the elect — and then again they may not. There is not too much hope here! It appears that some of the New England Puritans believed that all children were born going to hell and that the regeneration of their hearts by the Holy Spirit was the only hope for parents. They believed that regeneration preceded faith.

I do believe their view of the relationship between faith and regeneration is correct. However, these views, disconnected from the idea of the covenant, tended to foster a negative view of children. In the mind of some, children are nothing but unregenerate rascals (I think probably all parents have felt this way at times). I have read of at least one Puritan pastor who held to this view. When a young child died in his congregation he would use it as an

---

[8] *Westminster Confession of Faith*, The Publications Committee of the Presbyterian Church of Scotland (1976 Edition), Chapter X, Section III.

example to warn other young children that they too were going to die. He would show them how they were physically well-sized to fit into the coffin and how they could die anytime. Then he would warn the young children in his church about the danger of hell. All I can say to this is that I'm glad he was not my pastor.

The last view of the place of children in the church that I will deal with is the covenantal view. The Bible is not silent in regard to children. Actually, it says a great deal about children. When the Bible does speak of children, most often it is in the context of the covenant. Christians have covenant promises in regard to their children that God will work in their hearts and bring them to understand the gospel. The covenant teaches Christian parents that God has promised to regenerate their children and this will be evidenced by their conversion. Usually, it will happen over a period of time preceded by such things as prayer for the children, training and teaching them in the Christian faith, and parents being models of the Christian faith in their own lives.

Baptism is the sign and seal (assurance) given by God that this change in the hearts of our children will occur. Thus, Presbyterians baptize their children as infants with the expectation that either God has already regenerated their hearts, or he will regenerate their hearts. The writers of the Westminster Confession said it well when they wrote the following:

> The efficacy of baptism is not tied to that moment of time wherein It is administered; yet notwithstanding, by the right use of this ordinance, the grace promised is not only offered, but really exhibited and conferred by the Holy Ghost, to such (whether of age or infants) as that grace belongeth unto, according to the counsel of God's own will, in his appointed time.[9]

Baptism is efficacious. In other words, it works.

Baptism's efficacy in the hearts of the children may not happen at the time of baptism. God promises to regenerate their hearts at the time of their baptism, even though that regeneration may take

---

[9] Ibid. Chapter XXVIII, Section VI.

place either before or after their baptism. The promise is not only exhibited (displayed) by the sacrament in itself, but according to the language of the Confession, it is actually *conferred* at that time also. What does conferred mean? A college graduate has a degree conferred upon him at the time of his graduation. The degree grants to the graduate all the rights and privileges that come with that degree. That degree will open many doors for the graduate. Similarly, at baptism the child of the covenant has the rights conferred upon him that belong to all Christians. It is now official.

Notice too that the Confession says that it will take place in all those to whom this grace belongs. This takes us back to the mysterious doctrine of election that I described in Chapter 2. Ultimately, we know that baptism is effectual only for the elect, whether adults or children. However, I believe that the promises of God in the covenant should be at the forefront during the time of covenant baptism and not the complexities of the doctrine of election. In regard to the doctrine of election there is a time to speak about it, and there is a time to be silent about it.

Yes, ultimately all things must be left to the mysteries of God, but let's be sensitive to the needs of the parents. What they need to hear at the time of covenant baptism are the promises of God and not the mysteries that surround the doctrines of election. I know too many Reformed pastors that are haunted by what I call the "if clause." Every time they speak of a promise of God they believe they must add the phrase "if you are a true Christian" or "if you really believe." Well, this may be true, but sometimes the sure promises of God can die a slow death by a thousand qualifications, the most prominent being the "if clause."

I have listed these various views of the children in the church to distinguish the practical results of the covenant view from other views. We shall look more at covenant baptism in the next chapter. Now, we will look at a more precise definition of a covenant so that we may understand how the covenant view is developed in the Bible and how it relates to our children and their baptism.

What Is a Covenant?

The word covenant is used in several different ways in the Bible. Sometimes it is used in a more general way as simply an agreement between two or more persons. Often it signifies merely a contractual agreement. For example, in 1 Kings 5:12, Solomon made a contract with Hiram, the King of Tyre, to deliver timber for building the Temple in Jerusalem. Solomon agreed to pay him for the timber over a period of time (the installment plan). There were conditions upon both parties in this agreement. Hiram had to supply Solomon with the wood and Solomon had to pay Hiram for his work. This agreement was called a covenant. "The Lord gave wisdom to Solomon, just as He promised him, and there was peace between Hiram and Solomon, and the two of them made a covenant."

However, most often the word covenant as it relates to salvation is used in a more technical sense. Simply put, a covenant is God's promise (or bond) of salvation sealed in blood to you and your children, attached with a visible sign. Palmer Robertson in his book *The Christ of the Covenants* shortens the definition to "a bond-in-blood sovereignly administered."[10] Now, let's begin to dissect this definition of a covenant looking at three particular parts in this chapter.

Part #1- Who Is God?

First, we need to know something about the nature of God. God appears in space, time, and history (which he created). The Bible begins by assuming the existence of God and the fact that he created the world. Before the world was created, God was there. He was always there because he is infinite and eternal. Now try to grasp that! Maybe it is as difficult as trying to grasp the doctrine of election. After creation we have recorded in the Bible the fall of

---

[10] O. Palmer Robertson, *The Christ of the Covenants* (Phillipsburg, N. J.: P & R, 1980), 15.

mankind into sin through the disobedience of Adam and Eve. This plunged all mankind into a state of sin and misery eventually resulting in both spiritual and physical death.

The God who created the world then came forth with a promise to deliver man from his sin and misery. Thus, the premise of a covenant assumes the existence of a God that created the world, that the world fell into sin, and that this God announced the good news of the gospel to deliver man from his sin and misery. This good news (the gospel) was given in the form of a covenant. At this point, all I am trying to do is to show that before we can understand a covenant, we must first understand who God is and what happened at the beginning of the world.

Part #2 - God the King Makes A Promise

Secondly, we need to understand that a promise by God is a crucial part of the nature of a covenant. Notice too, that this promise was given by a sovereign self-existent God. It was not some agreement between man and God about how to be saved. It was not a mere negotiated contract between two or more persons. It was sovereignly administered by God who is a *King*. Covenantal language leads us to think of God as we would think of a King who rules all things by the power of his own will and desire. This is what the word sovereign means.

No one can challenge God. No one can make a deal with God. God decrees all things by the power of his own will and nothing can change that. If this is not the character of God then God is not God. A God who is not sovereign over all is no God at all. Thus, a covenant assumes that we understand God in this way. The most popular, modern view of God implies that he is only partially God because he is limited by man's will. This denigrates the personhood of God.

It is difficult especially for Americans to understand God as a sovereign King. We are not familiar with kings. We have been raised in a democracy (actually a constitutional republic) without kings, and we do not understand the nature of a true king. Our culture has sadly defined a new god — even our Christian God — and he is more of a democratic God than he is a sovereign King. And so the modern idea of salvation goes as follows: God votes and we vote, and ultimately our vote determines what God can and cannot do. God has been democratized.

We must change our view of God! Think of living in a country that was conquered by a king from another nation. That king has total power to do as he pleases. He does not convene a council and ask for our opinion on how he should rule our country. He is the conqueror. We are the conquered. He delivers to us a document (in writing) of life and death. Follow these laws and you shall live. Disobey and you shall die. Thus, the idea of a covenant begins with the understanding that it is a promise given to us in a document by a sovereign king. He is not our co-partner in a contractual agreement. We do not negotiate anything with the king. He sets the terms of life and death and we simply receive them with reverence.

Man fell into sin and death in the Garden of Eden, and God condescends to us as a sovereign king with a covenant that speaks of recovery from that life of misery and death. It tells us about the path to security — to health and life. He has it written in the form of a book which we now call the Bible. Understanding God as a sovereign King is necessary to understanding the nature of a covenant.

We know that the promise will be kept because of the integrity of the one who makes the promise. God is the God of truth. He cannot lie. His promises are true altogether. His promises are true forever. He makes promises in his covenant that are forever sure.

Part #3 - God's Promise Is Sealed in Blood

Thirdly, the covenant can be considered as more than a promise of peace from a King. In addition to the promise, the covenant also is a bond *sealed with blood*. There must be blood for there to be a covenant. When I was a young boy, it was common for boys my age to become blood brothers. This was a special bond. It created a unique and solemn relationship between me and another person. We would each cut a small place on our wrists and rub the two wrists together. Our blood would mix, or at least we thought they would. My blood was now running through his body and his through mine. Attendant with the sharing of blood there was usually a promise, for example, our keeping each other's secrets or being faithful to one another for life. It was similar to a biblical covenant because there was the flow of blood.

Conditions of the Covenant

It is also important to note that as it was with the agreement between Hiram and Solomon, the covenant is attached with conditions or expectations of both parties in the covenant. Some theologians prefer to include the conditions as part of the definition of a covenant, but, similar to Robertson's definition, I am not including the conditions as part of the definition in order to keep things simple.

For the first party, who is God, the covenant is conditioned upon his being faithful to his promises. Since God is God and he is a God of integrity, we know he will keep the conditions required of himself. In regard to the other party (us) there is a condition that we exercise faith in God. Faith that makes us right with God (just-ification) is not faithfulness. Faith is trusting in the promises of God and in nothing else for the forgiveness of our sins and for the blessings of God. Faith will bring forth a desire to be faithful to God. There are also sanctions attached to the conditions of the covenant. Keeping the covenant results in blessings (positive sanctions) and breaking the covenant results in cursing (negative sanctions).

Now, I want to mention something very special about God and the covenant. Don't forget it! It's really exciting. Even though faith on our part is a condition of the covenant, God regenerates us and by his grace implants that faith in our hearts. So, ultimately God guarantees the success of both parties of the covenant, both his part and our part. Because of this perspective, some theologians prefer to call the covenants of the Old and New Testaments the Covenant of Grace. When the covenant is viewed from God's perspective as the Covenant of Grace, it cannot fail on the part of either party because God guarantees his own integrity and God by his grace supplies believers with the faith required of them in the covenant agreement.

Old Testament Covenant - Genesis 15

We see the biblical nature of a covenant as we examine Genesis 15. God makes a promise to Abram (later called Abraham). As the Sovereign Creator of the world, God appeared to Abram and made a promise to him. "And he took him outside and said, 'Now look toward the heavens, and count the stars, if you are able to count them.' And he said to him, 'So shall your descendants be.' Then he believed in the LORD and He reckoned it to him as righteousness" (v. 5–6). Thus, here we have the first two parts of a covenant with conditions attached. We have God appearing to Abram as a King and making a promise of blessing that he would be the father of many nations. These are two parts of a covenant, the kingship of God and the promise that was made.

Notice also that the whole event was sealed in blood. "So he said to him, 'Bring Me a three-year-old heifer, and a three-year-old female goat, and three-year-old ram, and a turtledove, and a young pigeon.' Then he brought all these to Him and cut them in two, and laid each half opposite the other, but he did not cut the birds" (v. 9–10). This is the third part of the nature of a covenant — the shedding of blood.

We find later in the text that God appeared as a smoking oven and a flaming torch passing between the parts of the animal halves. By doing this God was saying if he did not keep his promises then may the same happen to him as happened to these animals. This was God's bond. This was a sign given to assure Abram that God would keep his promises. It was a promise made by a king sealed in blood with sanctions that if God did not keep his promises he would bring death upon himself.

In regard to Genesis 15, notice that God calls the ordeal the making of a covenant. More literally it was the cutting of a covenant, probably referring to the cutting of the animals. "On that day the LORD made a covenant with Abram…" (v. 18). Again, notice the major parts of a covenant that will be seen again in the Bible. A sovereign King appears to his subjects and makes a promise of blessing and he seals it in blood. There is a condition on God's part and that condition is faithfulness. There is a condition on Abram's part in the making of the covenant, and that condition is faith.

However, as we study the Bible we soon learn that even though Abram believed and fulfilled the condition, yet the Holy Spirit enabled Abram to believe by regenerating his heart first (see the definitions in Chapter 2). This faith that justifies also is the same faith that will bear fruit (sanctification).

New Testament Covenant – Book of Hebrews

In the Book of Hebrews of the New Testament (New Covenant) the writer reiterates the same principles and uses the term New Covenant. In Hebrews 8 the writer speaks of the old and new covenants. "But now He has obtained a more excellent ministry, by as much as he is also the mediator of a better covenant, which has been enacted on better promises" (v. 6). The old covenant promises were generally limited to the Jews, but the promises of the new covenant are better because they include the Gentiles. The original promise to Abraham that he would be the father of many nations was fulfilled through his descendent Jesus Christ as the gospel under the New Covenant was being taken to the Gentiles (nations).

Although the old and new covenants contain the same elements, the new covenant is so much better because it is sealed with the blood of Christ rather than with the blood of goats and other animals. Notice again the importance of blood. "For if the blood of goats and bulls and the ashes of a heifer sprinkling those who have been defiled sanctify for the cleansing of the flesh, how much more will the blood of Christ, who through the eternal Spirit offered Himself without blemish to God, cleanse your conscience from dead works to serve the living God?" (Heb. 9:13–14).

Without getting into the details here of the text, just notice the repetition of the concept of a covenant from the Old Testament. There is a sovereign King (Jesus) who makes promises and there is blood. This is why it is called a covenant. The gospel comes to us in the form of a covenant. God's promises of blessing (salvation) are sealed in the blood of Christ. As God regenerates his people they believe in Christ, and as they believe (fulfill their part of the covenant conditions) they are justified before God. The righteousness of God is imputed to them. Thus, my definition of a covenant (both in the Old and New Covenants) so far includes the three major parts of 1) a sovereign king, 2) promises or bond, and 3) the shedding of blood. In addition there are conditions and sanctions (blessings and curses) as the terms of the covenant are either kept or broken.

There are two more ingredients that make a covenant a true covenant. They include the fact that the children of believers are also recipients of the promises. Also, included in the nature of a covenant is the fact that a *visible sign* is given to all those who are recipients of the covenant promises including the children of believers. I will call these the *fourth* and *fifth* characteristics of a covenant. This brings us to the concept of covenant baptism. I will discuss this further in the next chapter.

5

COVENANT CHILDREN AND COVENANT BAPTISM

Introduction

Thus far we have covered three characteristics of a covenant. There must be a King, a promise (bond), and blood. The conditions of a covenant include faithfulness on God's part and faith on our part. God regenerates the hearts of believers so that they will believe and be able to keep the condition of having faith. As I mentioned in the last part of the previous chapter there are two other attributes in the definition of a covenant. These are often lost when men teach about the covenant. Thus far, we have seen that a covenant is a promise (bond) sovereignly administered in blood by a King. This promise in regard to our salvation is the gospel.

Now, we will look at the two other facets of a biblical covenant. Notice also that a covenant includes the fact that *fourthly* the promises are made to the children of adults who themselves are recipients of the promises of the covenant; and *fifthly*, these promises are accompanied with a visible sign to give further assurance that the promises both unto the adults and their children will come true. The sign assures us that the promises cannot be broken. We will now turn our attention to these two additional and important parts of a covenant.

Part #4:
Old Testament Promises to Children

The promises of the covenant of salvation always include the children of believers. In Genesis 17:7 we read "And I will establish My covenant between me and you and your descendents [seed] after you throughout their generations for an everlasting covenant, to be God to you and to your descendants after you." Yes, in

Galatians 3, Paul identifies the seed as Christ, but this does not nullify the fact that within the framework of the covenant promises of God as it works out in history, the seed also refers to the natural children of believers.

Moses later reminded the children of Israel that they were the recipients of the covenant promises of God which were originally made with Abraham, Isaac, and Jacob. "But you shall remember the Lord your God, for it is He who is giving you power to make wealth, that He may confirm His covenant which He swore to your fathers, as it is this day" (Deut. 8:18). When the Israelites were crying to be delivered from Egypt, the Bible says "So God heard their groaning; and God remembered His covenant with Abraham, Isaac, and Jacob. God saw the sons of Israel and took notice of them" (Ex. 2:24–25).

The Psalmist reminds us of the covenant promise that God made with Isaac and Jacob simply because they were the seed of Abraham. "He has remembered His covenant forever, the word which He commanded to a thousand generations, and the covenant which He made with Abraham and His oath to Isaac. Then He confirmed it to Jacob for a statute, to Israel as an everlasting covenant…" (Psalm 105:8–10). Notice that the covenant promise is confirmed to each generation. Some people call this covenant renewal. There are also those in the church today who believe that under the New Covenant the worship every Lord's Day is a covenant renewal.

To confirm a covenant is not to make a new covenant, but simply to call attention to what already exists. The covenant continues from generation to generation and is ultimately fulfilled in Christ; and is also fulfilled in all those who identify with Christ.

For those in Christ under the New Covenant, the covenant also includes their children. For this reason, it is also called an everlasting covenant. It began with Abraham and it extends into the New Testament, even to the end of the ages. The covenant promises will be trustworthy even into all eternity. The point is that even though the covenant is ultimately a covenant made with Christ, the covenant promises are still made to those in Christ, to believers and their children in both the Old and New Testaments.

Part #4 Continued:
New Testament Promises to Children

In the New Testament we find the same promises to believers and to their children as we do in the Old Testament. On the day of Pentecost in Peter's sermon to the Jews, he said "For the promise is "[unto] to you and to your children, (hence the title of this book) as many as the Lord our God will call to Himself" (Acts 2:39). What promise? The promise that was made to Abraham (Old Covenant) and now is fulfilled in Christ (New Covenant).

When Peter speaks of how God called him to the city of Joppa to stay at the home of Cornelius, he reminds us of what God said to Cornelius. God told Cornelius that Peter would come to him and preach the "words to you by which you will be saved, *you and all your household* [emphasis mine]" (Acts 11:14). We see one fulfillment of this promise in Acts 18:8 where "Crispus, the leader of the synagogue believed in the Lord *with all his household* [emphasis mine]." God saves households and the promise of salvation to the children of believers is guranteed by the covenant promise, the same promise that was made to Abraham, Isaac, and Jacob under the Old Covenant. This does not change under the New Covenant. The covenant under the New Testament is the same covenant that God made with Abraham in the Old Testament, except it is better since it is sealed in the blood of Christ, and it includes both Jews and Gentiles.

It is interesting that the Apostle Paul called the children of the church "saints." He considered them as part of the people of God. For example, in the Book of Ephesians (see also Colossians 1:1–2; 3:20) he addresses the Church as "...the saints who are at Ephesus and who are faithful in Christ Jesus" (1:1). Later in the book he addresses the various categories of the saints including husbands, wives, servants, and even the children. He addresses the children as follows: "Children, obey your parents in the Lord, for this is right" (6:1). Paul addressed everyone in the visible church as saints — including the children. The word saint describes one who is separated unto God as part of his covenant people. Forget the modern term "saint" used in the Roman Catholic Church. In the books of Ephesians and Colossians every person in the church including the children was called a saint.

In the Book of Acts we are told that Paul and Barnabas taught the disciples in the church at Antioch for an entire year, and there the disciples were first called Christians. "And when he left for Tarsus to look for Saul; and when he had found him, he brought him to Antioch. And for an entire year they met with the *church* [emphasis mine] and taught considerable numbers; and the disciples were first called Christians in Antioch" (Acts 11:25–26). Surely, children as part of the household of adult believers were included in the church at Antioch and they too were called Christians. I find it ironic that Muslim children are called Muslims and Jewish children are called Jewish, but that Christians find it very difficult to call their own children Christians. I think this is because there has been a shift away from the doctrine of the covenant.

Also, In 1 Corinthians 7:14 Paul calls the children of believers *holy* [emphasis mine]. Even if only one parent of a child is a Christian, this still makes their children holy. "For the unbelieving husband is sanctified through his wife, and the unbelieving wife is sanctified through her husband; for otherwise your children are unclean, but now they are holy." We all know that the word holy here does not mean perfect in character without sin. God forbid! Any parent can testify to this. However, children of believers are different than the children of unbelievers, even if only one parent is a Christian. The difference of having at least one parent as a believer makes a child a part of the covenant people of God. God has a claim on the child's life and sets the child aside as a recipient of his covenant promises.

Peter provides a good example of how the covenant works. In his first Epistle, Peter is referring to Noah and the saving of eight persons in the ark. He notes that eight people, Noah and his wife and his three sons and their wives, were saved through the water. The ark is similar to the church today. It is our safety boat in a world under the judgment of God.

We are told in Genesis 7:1 that Noah was saved because he was a righteous man. Only Noah was recognized as righteous. "Then the Lord said to Noah, 'Enter the ark, you and all your household, for you *alone* I have seen to be righteous before Me in this time." The wife and children were not considered to be righteous like Noah, but since they were part of his household, they too were saved in the ark. Peter's point is that it works the same today (during the period of the New Testament church). "Corresponding to that, baptism now saves you…" (1 Peter 3:21). Under the New Covenant the children of believers have a place in the church just like the children of Noah did in the ark. They go through the water of baptism just like the children of Noah did.

Thus, it appears clear that under both the Old and New Covenants the children of believers are recipients of the promises of God and the signs of that promise — even though the children may not even yet be capable of professing faith in Christ.

Paul also speaks of the children of Israel being baptized into Moses when they crossed the Red Sea as they were being pursued by the Egyptian armies. In 1 Corinthians 10:2 Paul says that they were "all baptized into Moses, in the cloud and in the sea…" Even in the Old Testament the people of God were baptized. Paul's point here is that God was not well-pleased with Israel in the wilderness, even though they were baptized. They had to endure the negative sanctions that follow disobedience. However, this does not nullify the fact that the entirety of Israel was baptized. This included the children.

This should not surprise us. It should also help us to think in terms of baptism being administered to all the people of God, including both parents and their children. Moses was their immediate and visible savior. By his leadership the people of God were delivered from their enemies through the water. This included the children. Likewise, we as Christians are delivered from the judgment of world by going through the waters of baptism. Like Moses and the people of Israel, our children (even infants) follow us through the waters of baptism as we follow Christ.

I might add that to neglect the baptism of children is contrary to the nature of a covenant, yet I do believe that all children of believers are covenant children, regardless of whether the parents recognize it or not. This does not justify the neglect of baptism that God commands for his people and their households, but it does not negate the work that God can do in the children of all believers, including those who deny covenant baptism. God is so gracious!

Part #5:
Signs of the Covenant in the Old Testament

Lastly, the fifth and final element in the definition of a covenant is that the covenant is attached with some visible sign to the recipients of the covenant promises. There are several texts that demonstrate that this visible sign accompanies the covenant promises. In the Old Testament the visible sign was circumcision. The connection between the covenant and the sign are so close that sometimes the sign itself is called the covenant. Sometimes the sign is identified with the thing signified. This is why Peter said that "baptism saves," even though we ultimately understand that God saves his people by changing the hearts of men.

In the book of Genesis circumcision is a sign of the covenant. "This is My covenant, which you shall keep, between Me and you and your descendants after you; every male among you shall be circumcised. And you shall be circumcised in the flesh of your foreskin, and it shall be the sign of the covenant between Me and you. And every male among you who is eight days old shall be circumcised throughout your generations, a servant who is born in the house or who is bought with money from any foreigner, who is not of your descendants. A servant who is born in your house or who is bought with your money shall surely be circumcised; thus shall My covenant be in your flesh for an everlasting covenant" (Gen. 17:10–13).

The visible sign was to be administered to all those within the household including servants. Servants were considered part of the household whether they were servants by birth or by purchase. They were under the head of the house and therefore included in the covenant promises of God. If the servants were to be circumcised, then how much more should the children be circumcised?

Part #5 Continued:
Signs of the Covenant in the New Testament

We find the same principle in the New Testament, only in the New Testament the sign was changed to baptism. Paul compares baptism to circumcision in the Book of Colossians. "… in Him you were also circumcised with a circumcision made without hands, in the removal of the body of flesh by the circumcision of Christ; having been buried with Him in baptism, in which you were also raised up with Him through faith in the working of God, who raised Him from the dead" (Col. 2:11–12).

Again, without getting into the details of the text, just notice that Paul identifies baptism with circumcision. In some sense, as Christians we were circumcised when we were baptized. The two signs function to demonstrate the same truth. Even though circumcision was administered to males only, baptism includes both males and females (which is another factor that changes the old covenant into the new covenant).

On the Day of Pentecost as Peter was preaching, some Jews asked him how they could be saved. The men were concerned about their own souls, but surprisingly (or maybe not so surprisingly) Peter not only told them what they must do to be saved, but he added the fact that as God saves them, he would also save their households. "Peter *said* to them, 'Repent, and each of you be baptized in the name of Jesus Christ for the forgiveness of your sins; and you will receive the gift of the Holy Spirit. For the promise is for you and *your children* [emphasis mine] and for all who are far off, as many as the Lord our God will call to Himself'" (Acts 2:38–39). The promise was the same promise made to Abraham and, as should be expected, it included the children of each household where there was a response in faith by a parent.

In Acts 16:14–15 we read "A woman named Lydia, from the city of Thyatira, a seller of purple fabrics, a worshiper of God, was listening and the Lord opened her heart to respond to the things spoken by Paul. And when she *and her household* [emphasis mine] had been baptized, she urged us, saying, 'If you have judged *me* [emphasis mine] to be faithful to the Lord, come into my house and stay.' And she prevailed upon us."

Notice, like Noah, only Lydia was judged to be faithful. She invited Paul into her household if he judged her alone to be faithful. The household was not required to pass that judgment by God. This implies that the household was baptized because of the faith of the mother. There is no reference to some profession of faith on the part of the members of the household. Simply notice that as Lydia became part of the covenant family of God by faith, her children (which could have included servants as well as infants) also became part of the covenant of God as Lydia did. They too were baptized. They too received the sign of the covenant just like those in the Old Testament.

This pattern is repeated in a later portion of Acts 16. There Paul and Silas are in jail, but after a great earthquake they were able to escape. The prison guard was about to commit suicide because if his prisoners escaped, he knew that he would be put to death by those in authority over him. Paul pleaded with him not to commit suicide. The prison guard asked then "Sirs, what must I do to be saved?" (v. 30). Notice that he asked what he himself could do for his own personal salvation. He did not ask about anything for his family. We find the answer of Paul and Silas in the following. "They said, 'Believe in the Lord Jesus and you will be saved, *you and your household* [emphasis mine]'" (v. 31). Now, we know later in this case that Paul and Silas spoke the word of the Lord to him together with all who were in his house (v. 32). We also know that the rest of the household was baptized.

It could be argued that the rest of the household of the Philippian jailor included adults only and they too responded to the gospel as adults. However, when there is doubt to the meaning of a word in the Bible, then we must compare Scripture with Scripture. In the Old Testament the word *household* included the entire family. Children were to be circumcised when they were eight-days old (Gen. 17:12). An eight-day old child is an infant. Households most often included small children. The key point is that even before Paul and Silas knew who belonged to the jailor's household, Paul made a promise not only to the jailor but also to his household which according to the definition of the word could have very well consisted of children.

Some Christians like bumper stickers and billboards as avenues to spread the word of God. Too often I have seen only a portion of Paul's response in Acts 16:31 posted on billboards or on church signs! Often I see quoted "Believe on the Lord Jesus Christ and thou shalt be saved." Sadly, this is an abuse of the text. The part at the end of the text that says "you and your household" is often omitted. I have always thought that this portion of this Scripture verse was omitted because there was no understanding of the covenant. To me it is heart-breaking.

Connection to the Future

Before I conclude this chapter, I think it is important to mention another point about the nature of a covenant. I think it is generally true that for my generation, salvation has become mainly centered on the individual and his relationship with God. We are saved from sin and we live on earth as aliens. We are different from the world. Our goal is to go to heaven. There is truth to all of this, but there is more.

From a covenantal view, salvation looks for God to work in the lives of our children and our children's children. It has a future aspect on this earth. It also is corporate. It pertains to groups such as families and nations. It is not just a way to escape the world we live in, but a basis for hoping that God will change the world we live in. He will do this through the generations that follow us as he blesses them. As the Second Commandment says, God will show "lovingkindness to thousands [of generations], to those who love me and keep My commandments" (Ex. 20:6). History began before we were born and it will not end when we die. The idea of a covenant is realistic about our own death, but it looks toward the future because it is a promise to thousands of generations not yet born.

There is a future for our children on earth after our death. We must live with an eye on the world that we will leave to our children. The Psalmist put it all together in Psalm 103:15–18.

> "As for man, his days are like grass; as a flower of the field, so he flourishes. When the wind has passed over it, it is no more, and its place acknowledges it no longer. But the lovingkindness of the Lord is from everlasting to everlasting on those who fear Him, and His righteousness to children's children, to those who keep His covenant and remember His precepts to do them."

Conclusion

This concludes the five part definition of a covenant. I believe I have covered the main Scripture passages to demonstrate its nature. *A covenant is a promise in blood given by a king that includes the children and is accompanied with a visible sign administered to the entire household.* The promise is as good as the integrity of the one who makes the promise. God is trustworthy and we should expect him to keep his promises. The more you ingrain this definition into your mind the more it will become part of your life as you read the Bible. The first thing you know, you will be using the concept of a covenant to interpret all of the Bible. This is good. The word covenant will become part of your biblical vocabulary and then part of your mind as you read the Bible. You will filter all the texts of the Bible through the concept of a covenant. It will change how you read the Bible. If you do that, then I have accomplished part of what I wanted in this book.

As I alluded to before, we all approach the Bible with certain assumptions. Many Christians in America approach the Bible with the idea that Jesus died to save everyone and that our salvation is dependent on our making a decision for Jesus. God is holding out his hand hoping all of us will respond, but ultimately the decision is our decision as adults. Salvation is mostly a democratic response in accepting God's offer. Children are too small to respond and therefore are left out of the picture until they reach the age of accountability. This is not my approach. This is not a covenantal approach.

I have given you an alternative approach by introducing you to the covenant. Salvation is not only personal but corporate. God not only works with individuals but he works through families. He therefore is operative in the salvation of our children from the time of their birth or even from the time they are in the womb. God is sovereign and because of this we have hope for our children. These are two different approaches to salvation and to the word of God.

At this point, before I go on to the next chapter, I will answer below some common questions that arise when Christians are first introduced to the idea of the covenant.

Some Common Questions

Question regarding Election

Question: If certain people are not elect, then does this nullify the promises of the covenant?

Answer: No. Remember that the doctrine of election is a mysterious doctrine that we will never understand while we are on this earth. "The secret things belong to the Lord our God, but the things revealed belong to us and to our sons forever, that we may observe all the words of this law" (Deut. 29.29). There are questions about election we just cannot answer even though we should take advantage of the jewels of truth we derive from it. The doctrine of election was given to us to show that our salvation is dependent on

God and not on ourselves. We are saved entirely by the grace of God (Eph. 1). It was also given to us to explain what appear to be failures on the part of God's promises (Rom. 9). It appears that the Jews rejected Christ and that God was not in control, but Paul basically says — not so fast. It was all predestined by God.

The doctrine of election was not given to us in order to nullify the promises of God. Rather than nullify the promises of God, in one sense the doctrine of election guarantees the promises of God. Because God is all powerful, we can be sure that he can carry out his promises. This actually gives us greater hope in the promises of God for our children because we know God can keep his promises. God can change their hearts. and we will spend much time at the throne of grace pleading for God to keep his promises, reminding him that he is a covenant God. My advice is as follows. Focus on the benefit of the doctrine of election and avoid the confusing thoughts about it that we were never intended to understand. It glorifies God, and it provides an answer to the dilemma when the promises of God appear to fail; but it was never intended to denigrate the covenant promises of God and their benefit to the people of God.

Question regarding Rejection

Question: If it turns out that one of my children rejects Christ, then should I just treat them as one of God's non-elect?

Answer: Never give up on your children as long as there is life. The prodigal son rejected his inheritance, but later came to his senses. Our children may go through rebellion, struggles, and doubt, but we have a special hope that as we have raised them in the fear and admonition of the Lord, then they too will come to their senses and come to Christ.

Question regarding Profession

Question: If children are baptized as infants, must they make a profession of faith themselves later on in life?

Answer: Covenant children are expected to make their own profession of faith when they come to understand the gospel. Before they can be admitted to the Lord's Supper, they must make a credible profession of faith before the elders of the church. They will be asked to stand before the congregation and affirm that their only hope is in Christ. Once children are baptized as infants, then one of the goals of parents is to look forward to the day when their children will make their own profession of faith and be admitted to the Lord's Supper. This will be part of the evidence that God has been faithful to his covenant promises when they were baptized as infants. Actually, this should be a special day in the life of the family and the church. It should be a day of celebration.

Question regarding Withdrawal

Question: Is it true that all I have to do is have my children baptized, and then just let God to do the rest?

Answer: Absolutely not. God is under no obligation to keep his covenant promises and change the hearts of your children apart from raising of your children in the instruction in the Lord. I will deal with this question more in the next chapter, but unless we model the Christian faith before them, pray for them, and teach them the doctrines of our holy religion as we faithfully take them to church, then we should not expect to see their conversion. The amazing thing that we often see is that God is so gracious to save our covenant children even when the covenant parents are not as faithful as they should be to fulfill their own covenant responsibilities. This does not give us any excuse for our laxity, but just illustrates again how gracious our God is.

I've answered a few popular questions about the covenant and children. In the next chapter I will consider how our view of the covenant affects the way we raise our children.

6
RAISING COVENANT CHILDREN

Introduction

Does the covenant make a difference in raising children? The answer is yes. I would grant that most biblical principles regarding child-rearing are the same regardless of whether or not you recognize the covenantal status of your children. However, there is a difference. The difference will be most evident in your attitude toward your children and the hope that you have for them. There will be a difference in what you expect from applying the biblical principles of childrearing.

There are many good books about how to raise children from a biblical perspective. I won't try to add much to these. However, I will try to demonstrate how the covenant does make a difference in raising children. Then I will deal with a few basic principles that must be present in every Christian home if we are to properly raise our children in the Lord and expect God to work in their lives as he has in our own.

How the Covenant Affects Attitude

Children are adorable. Most children enjoy a good hug and like to give hugs back. Children are mostly as sweet as can be. However, anyone who has raised children soon learns that children can be rebellious and just downright ugly at times. They don't have to be taught to say "no." They already know how to do that. They don't have to be taught how to be selfish. I'm always a little tickled when young Christian parents learn just how sinful their children can be. Never did they expect this!

Covenant parents also know that in raising their children in the fear and admonition of the Lord, that God can use their efforts to bring about a heart change in their children. Yes, ultimately it is the Holy Spirit that must change the heart, but the Holy Spirit uses the means that God ordains. Most often God uses common, ordinary, and even mundane means to do his supernatural work. It is the same way with adults. Remember, the mundane is an instrument of God too. God works through means. The Holy Spirit must bring about change in us, but the Spirit does not work apart from the means of God's word. Likewise, the covenant teaches us that the Holy Spirit most often works through the parents to bring about real and lasting change in the hearts of their children.

Covenant parents who have their children baptized have a hope that non-covenant parents do not have. Remember, as parents submit their children to the sacrament of baptism, a Sovereign God is making a promise to the parents that he will be the God of their children. Baptism is a sign and seal of this promise. Covenant baptism is not accepting baptism on behalf of our children. It is not receiving the benefits of baptism in their place. I'm not sure where this idea came from. Contrary to this view, baptism as a sign and a seal is the affirmation of the veracity of the one behind the seal, namely God. If you receive a letter from the President of the United States, you need to look for the seal on the letter to make sure it is genuine. Likewise, the seal of baptism guarantees the reality and integrity of God who orders the baptism of children. The seal makes sure that these promises are good and they are from God.

A Wet Dedication Service?

Neither is baptism merely a "wet-dedication" service. It is not a dedication service with water where children are dedicated to God like Samuel was in the Old Testament (1 Sam. 1:28). The word dedicate does not capture the weight of the meaning of the word covenant. Maybe a simple dedication service that exists in some churches satisfies the covenant need of non-covenant parents to have God bless their children? Just a thought!

The third question in the Book of Church Order of the Presbyterian Church in America (PCA) asks parents if they are willing to dedicate their children to God (see Appendix).

I must make a confession. For most of my forty-two year tenure as a pastor in the PCA I have refrained from using the word "dedicate" in the third vow required in the administration of infant baptism. I've dedicated a church building, but I have never asked parents to dedicate their child in covenant baptism. The third vow reads:

> "Do you now unreservedly *dedicate* [emphasis mine] your child to God, and promise, in humble reliance upon divine grace, that you will endeavor to set before (him) a godly example, that you will pray with and for (him), that you will teach (him) the doctrines of our holy religion, and that you will strive, by all the means of God's appointment, to bring (him) up in the nurture and admonition of the Lord?"

In my personal copy of the BCO I have a line drawn through the word "dedicate" and placed the verb "present" above it as a substitute. I use the word "present" at every infant baptism I perform. "Do you now unreservedly present your child to God...."

Admittedly, the second vow speaks of "God's covenant promises." Even with the surrounding language, it seems to me that the word "dedicate" is a compromise with our non-covenantal brethren. They dedicate. We baptize. I am afraid that in many PCA churches covenant baptism has become little more than a wet dedication service.

The popular justification for the dedication of children is from 1 Samuel 1:28 where the NASV says that Hannah "dedicated" Samuel to the Lord. The KJV uses the words "lent to the Lord." So much for the newer translations! Samuel was not raised by his parents. When Samuel was "dedicated" he lived with Eli the Priest "as a boy" in order to minister to the Lord. He was taken away from his parents. This is quite different from a child being raised by Christian parents.

Infant baptism is not primarily a promise of parents to God, but first and foremost a promise of God to the parents. If there is any dedication, God is dedicating himself to his oath to be a God to both the parents and to the child. It is true that parents are bound by oath to raise the child according to the principles of God's word, but this is not a dedication. It is a conditional covenant promise on the part of the parents.

The influence of non-covenant churches is so great in our society that the word "dedicate" will generally be interpreted within the paradigm of their theology, regardless of how much we guard the meaning of the word "dedicate" with other words. It is interesting to note that the infant baptismal vows used in the both Orthodox Presbyterian Church (OPC) [see Appendix] and the Associate Reformed Presbyterian Church (ARP) do not use the word "dedicate."

Maybe this haggling over words is minor, but for me it is a matter of conscience. It's also a matter of the importance of the covenant when the landscape of America is covered with non-covenant churches. The ramifications of the covenant go much further than infant baptism. They go to the heart of how to raise children born into the church. This is another reason for this book.

Baptism – A Means of Grace

Baptism is a sacrament where grace is present. It is a sacred act whereby God affirms that he will be a God to our children as he has been to us. God is giving assurance to the parents. This grace promised in the sacrament should eventually become visible as we see our children look to Christ as their only hope in this world and the world to come. When the regeneration of their hearts will happen or whether it has already happened, we do not know. However, because of their baptism, we look upon our children with hope and great expectation as a result of the promises of God. We have something to rejoice about. Even on our worst days when we are about to pull our hair out because of their bad behavior, we can go to God and remind him of his promises. We can plead with God before the throne of grace to be faithful to his covenant promises.

We can bring our case before God as a good lawyer does before a judge.

Because we are covenantal, we do not hold the cold attitude that our children "may be elect or they may not be elect," and that there is really nothing we can do about it. As I previously mentioned, some Calvinistic parents just hope that their children are among the elect. Just like covenant parents, they pray a lot too, but they lack a hope in the promises of God. On bad days even covenant parents may be tempted to give up any hope for their children and just declare them reprobate, but this is never the attitude that God intended that covenant parents have toward their children.

It is also important to notice that we do not have the attitude of some parents who believe they should just wait on their children to make their own decision when they reach the age of accountability. This hope revolves around the idea that when their children grow older they will make a profession of faith as a response to an altar call or some other type of pressure (often at Church Camp). In these families, most Bible instruction received by the children will come from the Church Sunday School or Youth Group. Little instruction comes from the home. Once they make their profession of faith by walking the aisle or raising their hand, then these parents will be assured of the salvation of their children. They will be baptized and all will be well with their souls. This may not be a fair caricature of all non-covenant parents, but it does represent a considerable number.

How the Covenant Affects Attitude

Maybe now you see how the covenantal perspective makes a difference in the way we approach our children. We don't tell our children that they are little rascals and unless they change they are going to hell. We don't tell them that they need to examine themselves to see if they are among the elect. Neither do we push them into making a decision for Jesus at some young age when they have no depth of understanding about the things of God. No, we train them in the fear and admonition of the Lord as long as they are under our headship. We bring them up as part of the body of Christ, expecting God to work in their hearts as he has in our own. This gives parents a positive attitude toward their children and it gives them hope.

It has been my experience that covenant-oriented childrearing works. In the church where I was a pastor for thirty-one years, with few exceptions, where parents were faithful to their covenant vows, and where there was diligence in instruction both at home and at church with discipline and prayer, the small children inevitability became mature adult believers. The detection of a saving faith came at different times. Sometimes early and sometimes late! I think some of them were still coming to a saving knowledge of Christ even after they moved somewhere else as adults. After growing up and leaving home, very often they came back as committed believers in Christ.

Now, this hopeful attitude toward our covenant children does not negate the necessity of both teaching and training them. As a matter of fact it increases the recognition that this *must* be done because it is through these parental responsibilities that God works faith into their hearts. The covenant promises do not negate biblical instruction and discipline in the Lord. As a matter of fact, it is because we do teach them God's word that we have this hope for them. Admittedly, in the past some Presbyterian churches assumed that all they had to do was baptize their children and all was well. As I mentioned before, this attitude may have contributed toward many empty pews in many Presbyterian churches. Without an aggressive plan to teach and discipline covenant children, the promises of baptism will fail.

Principles and Application

What then is needed in raising our children so that we can expect God to work in their hearts and keep his promises sealed in their baptism? We must raise them in the fear and admonition of the Lord (Eph. 6:4). As I mentioned before, there have been many good books written on how to raise children according to biblical principles, but I will mention a few main principles in this chapter that are essential. There are thousands of situations that a parent must deal with, and I can't deal with them all. However, if we have a few basic principles, we can deduce from those principles an answer that will help us in regard to just about any situation we face on any particular day.

Seminary prepared me for much in the ministry, but later when I was out on the field as the pastor of a church, there were numerous situations that I remember thinking — they did not teach me about this in seminary. This was especially true in counseling. While I was in the pastorate, I dealt with many situations never mentioned in all of my counseling courses, or even in all the books that I had read on counseling. However, what I did learn is that if you have some basic biblical principles in your head that most every situation can be handled by applying those principles.

Therefore, even though I saw things I never thought I would see, I was not overwhelmed. I knew I had the basic principles of the Bible in my mind, and that I could apply those principles to just about any pastoral situation that I faced. This gave me confidence. The same is true in raising covenant children.

What is Love?

It would be rather simplistic and trite for me to say that what you need to do is to *love* your children. The word "love" has lost its biblical content today. I'm not sure if many people in our own culture even understand the meaning of the word love. Hollywood has destroyed its meaning. Most of what is called love today is merely infatuation or anything that contributes to personal self-esteem.

In the Bible love is sacrifice. For God so loved the world that he gave — he did not take. We don't hear much of that. Therefore, I will mention three characteristics of biblical love that must be present in the life of parents if they are to see God work in the lives of their children. This is not to say that there are not more, but again if you have these principles in your head, and you have the wisdom to apply them, then you will be on your way to seeing God bless your children. You will be on your way to being able to handle most any situation that arises.

The Principle of Modeling

The first principle that covenant parents need to know is the fact that the parents must model the Christian faith in their own lives. The second and third principles that I have selected are also necessarily correlated — firmness and kindness. I suppose that firmness and kindness are just applications of the responsibility of modeling, but they are important enough in my mind to detach them and deal with each of them separately below.

Parental Modeling

First, parents must model the Christian faith in their own lives. This does not mean that parents must be perfect because perfection does not exist in us. However, no matter how firm and kind you are with your children, if you do not model the Christian faith in your own life you may very well lose your children.

Children need to see Christ in you. By this I mean a love of Christ which results in the fruit of the spirit. "But the fruit of the Spirit is love, joy, peace, patience, kindness, goodness, faithfulness, gentleness, self-control; against such things there is no law" (Gal. 6:22–23). Notice that kindness is mentioned here and is part of the modeling quality. Now again, remember that perfection is unattainable, but all Christians should exhibit these qualities to some degree.

My purpose is not to put parents on a guilt trip. However, remember this: who you are is more important than what you do. If you are a child of God and love Christ sincerely, then what you do in raising your children will be guided mostly by who you are rather than by some book of instructions on what to do in any situation. Most parents would like to have a "Child-Rearing Manual" to deal with any and every situation, but I have not seen one yet.

Children also need to hear about Christ from their parents — all the time! There must be a Christian world-and-life view in the home. Christian parents must interpret everything by reference to the Word of God. The Christian faith is not a Sunday-only event. It is the center — the fulcrum of all of life. "You shall teach them diligently to your sons and shall talk of them when you sit in your house and when you walk by the way and when you lie down and when you rise up" (Deut 6:7). Our children must be saturated with the word of God. Parents must constantly be interpreting all of life in light of God's word. If at all possible, covenant parents should either home school or send their children to a Christian School.

Using the Imitation Factor

Children love to imitate. Covenant children will tend to imitate their parents. This fruit of the Spirit in your life is contagious. Children will tend to pick up these traits and imitate them.

I remember as a young father how I was thrilled, but yet alarmed, when I saw one of my sons wanting to imitate his father. I would cut the grass in my yard with a push lawn-mower, and nothing would do him but to have his own toy lawn-mower and follow my steps as I cut the grass. It was quaint, but it was more than that. I knew that he would seek to imitate me in all the other areas of life, and I had better be on my toes.

Set a pattern for your children to imitate. What do children see in you? What do they recognize about their parents? When they are asked about Mom and Dad, hopefully they can inform others that Mom and Dad go to church regularly. Mom and Dad worship God. They listen to the sermons and they sing the hymns. Mom and Dad love worship. If it is important to Mom and Dad, it will be important to the children. There is no greater blessing for me as a pastor than to see parents singing with gusto in a worship service with their children standing beside them trying to imitate, even though some of them cannot even read yet.

Children's church does not contribute toward family worship, so at the right age they need to be in worship sitting beside Mom and Dad. We must form habits in our children, and then we must pray that God will work the fruit of his Spirit into them as they learn those habits. As you love your neighbor and as you show mercy to the needy, your children will be watching. Hey, it works! As a pastor, I've seen it work over and over.

Children know if you are real. They can detect a hypocrite a thousand miles away. They know when you love Christ more than anything else in the world, even more than them. When they see this, the impact will be so great that it will actually work toward changing the hearts of your children. Modeling is a powerful tool of God in changing the hearts of children.

Two More Qualities

Firmness and kindness are the second and third qualities that parents need. Both are important. One without the other is destructive. Firmness without kindness is harsh. Kindness without firmness is mush. There must be a good balance between the two. Many parents go too far one way or the other. Too much law without grace or too much grace without law is not good for the soul! I suppose we are all off-balance, but we need to seek a moderate mid-point between the two as we busy ourselves in raising our children.

The Principle of Firmness

Let me deal with the necessity of firmness first. Parents must develop in their children a respect for authority, especially their own. They must develop the ability to demand and see a proper response from their children. For some adult personalities this is

difficult. Some parents are just not commanding by personality. In
the pastorate I had to confront a few parents about the need to be
more commanding. There should be a certain amount of fear in the
hearts of the children if they do not properly respond. As Christians
have a healthy fear of God, so children should have a healthy fear of
their parents. Too much mush and not enough fear may produce
disrespectful and manipulating children. Their crying and moaning
may be just pure rebellion. There needs to be a command response
from children. You command and they respond by obeying. Some
children are more difficult than others. Some are more "strong-
willed" and will present a greater challenge. However, the principles
are the same.

Now, how is this command-response developed? Let me
mention a few things you can do:
- Speak firmly.
- Look them in the eye and speak with all seriousness. No
  squirming allowed.
- Sit them in a chair and tell them they must be quiet and
  cannot get up until you tell them to get up.
- When all else fails, then spank.

First, you need to develop the "voice of authority." It has a
distinct sound. Children know it when they hear it. It is not screaming, but it is firm. They also know that if they do not respond
correctly, they will see steps two through four above. Some parents
move directly to step four — spanking.

Parents have to be clear and consistent. The children should
know the rules before you even speak. They know when you are
consistent. The worst thing you can do is change the rules in the
middle of the game. This is what the Bible calls "exasperating your
children" (Eph 6:4). Once you tell them that playing in their food is
not acceptable, then it will always be that way — for all eternity. No
exceptions allowed!

If you are at the point where a firm and consistent command
does not get a command-response, then you move to the second
step. This second step is to look them in the eye, with a pointed
finger (if you choose) and speak like their response may result in a

more catastrophic event if they do not obey. Again, don't allow squirming. Don't be manipulated by crying, unless the crying is evidence of repentance that guarantees immediate obedience. Repeated occurrences of disobedience are evidence of manipulation.

The third step (and some people skip this one) is to sit them in a "naughty chair." They know they must sit there until you are satisfied that it is time to get up. You might even want to set a timer on the kitchen stove. Again, no talking, no manipulating by crying, no playing with toys, and no iPads! This is a punishment. Call it "time-out" if you wish. Do not put them in a room by themselves. You can't watch them there. Put them in a chair in the room where you are and where you can see them. Often they will just fall asleep.

Step number four is spanking. If the other steps do not work, then the last resort is spanking. Spanking is an art in itself. You probably need to learn how to spank. Below is an article I wrote on an internet website some time ago that summarizes this process.

My Experience as a Parent

I raised several children and I spanked all of them. One thing I learned was that if I spanked them biblically, then I seldom had to spank them at all. Actually, over the years of their childhood, spankings were so minimal that I seldom remember spanking them at all. I've always said that if parents are spanking their children often then they are not spanking them properly. Spanking should be done sparingly and only after following other means of discipline first.

Now, of course, painful discipline was only a minor part of life in our home. On an average day, Daddy was everything from a four-legged horse to a tickle-monster. I knew how to have fun, and I enjoyed my children tremendously. Laughing and levity were a major part of our daily lives.

Because they had been spanked properly when it was needed, and also because Dad knew how to have fun with them, I was able to use other less painful methods of discipline on most occasions.

My first approach to necessary correction was what I called the voice. It was like God was speaking from heaven. A stern voice should defuse any further crisis. Then there was "the look." They knew by the stare in my eyes that they were in trouble. It was a stern stare where my eyes looked like two missiles ready to fire. At this point, I did not have to say a further word. I just had to give them the look. Never underestimate the power of the look! It is especially useful in public places.

If the stare did not work then there was the hot-seat (naughty chair). There was the "trail of tears" to the hot-seat. It was a march to the living-room with my right hand firmly gripped to their left hand. By this time they were usually crying because of guilt or fear — or maybe both. While we walked to the hot-seat, I told them in plain words what the offense was. The hot-seat was reserved for offenses like screaming, complaining, fussing, and other such daily rancor.

I made them sit down in the chair. It was a plain chair but because of the trouble they were in, it was a "hot-seat" too. I told them they were to sit there until I allowed them to get up. With a God-like voice I told them to quit crying. Soon, quietness permeated the whole house. Even the other siblings became quiet. Even Mom became quiet too. You could hear a pin drop. That was good. That was exactly what was needed — silence. Daddy was in control.

Lastly, after a period of time that suited me, I told them they could arise from the hot-seat. They knew that payment had been made for their trespasses and they were free. Life quickly returned to normal. Dad's look was gone. It would probably be a few more days (or maybe a few more hours) before this happened again.

Spanking was reserved for very serious offenses like lying, stealing, or contumacy (constant rebellion). It was a serious event in the household. None of this quick, fast hand to the bottom! No spanking in public. When I spanked my children it was like the holy and just God was paying a special visit to our house. I was upset, yet in control of myself. I used a rod — for me it was my belt. I took them to their bedroom, told them to drop their pants (or skirts), and I made sure two or three licks were very painful. They certainly did not want God to pay another special visit any time soon.

Of course, other methods may be appropriate at times such as mere diversion of attention or counting to five. However, the look and the hot-seat should be part of your arsenal in child-rearing.

The Principle of Kindness

Lastly, to see God bless your covenant children, there must of course be kindness. Firmness without kindness can be a type of brutality. I love the verse in Second Thessalonians where Paul speaks of the necessity of kindness in his ministry, "We urge you, brethren, admonish the unruly, encourage the fainthearted, help the weak, be patient with everyone" (1 Thess. 5:14). Notice that in this text that there is both firmness and kindness. Probably there is more kindness than firmness.

Paul is writing to Christian adults as they relate to one another, but these words can also be applied to parents raising children. Children are weak. It is the nature of being a child. They need a lot of gentleness. They need a lot of tenderness. Paul put it vividly in his first letter to the Thessalonians where speaking of his own ministry, he says, "But we proved to be gentle among you, as a nursing *mother* tenderly cares for her own children" (1 Thess. 2:7).

Children need encouragement. They tend to faint. You need to build courage into your children. You need to give them a lot of affirmation. You need to be there when they participate in activities, if at all possible. Encourage them when they do well and also encourage them when they don't do so well. Find out what they do well and encourage them to pursue excellence. Shower hugs and kisses all over them. Soften the blows they will receive in life.

The Most Important Gift

The greatest kindness you can give to your children is to ingrain in them the word of God. Teach them to memorize Scripture passages. Teach them the Child's Shorter Catechism. Time will be short and they will be grown and gone before you know it. Don't lose this precious time. Don't let them grow up ignorant of the things of God. The world will be seeking to capture their minds, but you need to make sure that they carry the sword of the Lord in their hearts. Memorization will pay off in the future.

Timothy was a covenant child and Paul reminded him how he had been taught the Bible from the time he was a child where he said, "…and that from childhood you have known the sacred writings which are able to give you the wisdom that leads to salvation through faith which is in Christ Jesus" (2 Tim. 3:15). God primarily works through his word and it is essential that children grow up knowing the Holy Scriptures from the time they are babes. In addition to instructing them at home, use the Sunday School class for your children if your church has one. Saturate them in the Word of God. Pray with them and for them. This is a responsibility that parents assume when their children are baptized.

A Warning For Older Children

When children grow older the methods may change somewhat. It's hard to spank a thirteen year old boy who is over six feet tall. During the teenage years, it is good to remind them of their covenant privileges and the danger of rejecting the covenant blessings of God. Covenant children have special blessings. Parents should remind them of that. They have been raised in a Christian home, and that is a great privilege granted by God. They have known the Holy Scriptures from the time they were children. They have seen the faith modeled by their parents. They have known both firmness and kindness.

Whenever I perceived any rebellion in my older children it was my practice to warn them of the danger of rejecting the covenant. The Jew was first in both blessing and in tribulation (Rom. 2:9–10). Likewise, for covenant children, we should tell them that since they have been so blessed by God, if they reject God, then God will come after them first in judgment. I would say to my children that God loves you, but if you reject God and go after the world, be sure God will get you! Let your children (especially the teenagers) know that they have been greatly blessed but if they reject the covenant, then God will deal with them harshly.

Conclusion

This concludes my short summary of the principles of raising covenant children. If you have the correct biblical principles in your mind, then you can probably apply them to almost any situation. There is no magic formula that fits every situation. Other parents who have been successful in raising their children may be your best resource for answers in difficult situations. However, remember that your own character is the best guarantee of changing your children into godly adults. If you are firm with them, chaos can be avoided. If you are kind and gracious with them, they will imitate those attributes eventually (don't give up!).

There is no greater joy than having covenant children and watching them grow into mature Christian adults because you have been a role-model for them, and because you have been both firm and kind. It is a satisfaction in old age that cannot be replaced with anything else on this earth.

I hope this book has been helpful. Parents need all the help and hope they can get. May you find strength in the blessings of the covenant promises of God signed and sealed at the baptism of your children! Remember, the covenant is the promise of God sealed in blood. Once you see your children flourishing in the faith, you will give all glory to God, and ultimately this is what it is all about.

APPENDIX
COVENANT BAPTISMAL VOWS

Book of Church Order
Presbyterian Church in America

1. Do you acknowledge your child's need of the cleansing blood of Jesus Christ, and the renewing grace of the Holy Spirit?
2. Do you claim God's covenant promises in (his) behalf, and do you look in faith to the Lord Jesus Christ for (his) salvation as you do for your own?
3. Do you now unreservedly dedicate your child to God, and promise, in humble reliance upon divine grace, that you will endeavor to set before (him) a godly example, that you will pray with and for (him), that you will teach (him) the doctrines of our holy religion, and that you will strive, by all the means of God's appointment, to bring (him) up in the nurture and admonition of the Lord?

Book of Church Order
Orthodox Presbyterian Church

1. Do you acknowledge that although our children are born in sin and therefore are subject to condemnation, they are holy in Christ by virtue of the covenant of grace, and as children of the covenant are to be baptized?
2. Do you promise to teach diligently to [name of child] the principles of our holy Christian faith, revealed in the Scriptures of the Old and New Testaments and summarized in the Confession of Faith and Catechisms of this Church?

3. Do you promise to pray regularly with and for [name of child], and set an example of piety and godliness before [him/her]?

4. Do you promise to endeavor, by all the means that God has appointed to bring [name of child] up in the nurture and admonition of the Lord, encouraging [him/her] to appropriate for [himself/herself] the blessings and fulfill the obligations of the covenant?

SUBJECT AND NAME INDEX

SCRIPTURE INDEX

www.ingramcontent.com/pod-product-compliance
Lightning Source LLC
Chambersburg PA
CBHW022034090426
42741CB00007B/1063